Steve,

It was great having you on the team — looking forward to many more good experiences with you in the future

Keith
Feb 2011

"*The Gifted Boss* reminds me of *The One Minute Manager*—a fast, entertaining read that shows a good manager how to move up to the next level. A 'must read' book." —ERIC CROWN, CEO, Insight Enterprises, Inc.

"Prepare yourself for a journey of discovery! Dale Dauten provides an entertaining yet thought-provoking look at why some companies are succeeding more than others in our ever-changing marketplace. If you've been wondering how to not just survive but to thrive in business in the coming years, this book is for you." —TOM HOPKINS, author of *How to Master the Art of Selling* and *Sales Prospecting for Dummies*™

"For those who have progressed from the business manager to a leader of people, you're not done yet! Dale Dauten is now challenging us to become a 'gifted boss' through this enchanting easy read. I found the book to be fun as well as enlightening and can't wait to practice what he preaches." —ROY VALLEE, Chairman and CEO, Avnet, Inc.

"Wow! Less is more. With this book Dale Dauten has pulled together the most vital wisdom on what it really takes to be a gifted boss. Read it, and your people will thank you." —PAUL G. STOLTZ, PH.D.; President and CEO, PEAK Learning, Inc.; author of *Adversity Quotient: Turning Obstacles into Opportunities*

"*The Gifted Boss* is another home run from gifted writer Dale Dauten. . . . No boss in America today will want to be without this compelling book on how to lead employees to greatness." —STEVE CHANDLER, author of *100 Ways to Motivate Yourself* and *Reinventing Yourself*

"*The Gifted Boss* provides new insights that will benefit any boss who wants to find and keep great employees as well as anyone looking for a great boss." —MICHAEL LEBOEUF, PH.D.; author of *How to Win Customers and Keep Them for Life* and *Working Smart*

The Gifted Boss

★ ★ ★ ★ ★

Also by Dale Dauten

The Max Strategy

Taking Chances

The Gifted Boss

How to Find, Create and Keep

Great Employees

★ ★ ★ ★ ★

Dale Dauten

William Morrow and Company, Inc.

NEW YORK

Library of Congress Cataloging-in-Publication Data

Dauten, Dale A.
The gifted boss : how to find, create and keep great employees /
by Dale Dauten.
p. cm.
ISBN 0-688-16877-9
1. Executive ability. 2. Executives. 3. Employees—Attitudes.
I. Title.
HD38.2.D38 1999
658.4'09—dc21   98-54390
CIP

Printed in the United States of America

16 17 18 19 20

BOOK DESIGN BY CATHRYN S. AISON

www.williammorrow.com

To three friends

who have raised my standards and my spirits...

Jim Fickess,

Richard Gooding and

Roger Axford

Success follows doing what you want to do.
There is no other way to be successful.
—MALCOLM FORBES

There are two kinds of talent,
man-made talent and God-given talent.
With man-made talent, you have to work very hard.
With God-given talent, you just touch it up once in a while.
—PEARL BAILEY

The Six Realities
of
Gifted Bosses and Great Employees

1. The "talent-squared" workplace is possible because gifted bosses and great employees want the same things from a workplace:
   - Freedom from . . .
     management,
     mediocrity and
     morons.
   - A change.
   - A chance.

2. Gifted bosses don't just hire employees, they acquire allies.

3. Great employees don't have jobs, they have talents. They enter the job market once (if at all), and thereafter their talents are spotted, courted and won over.

4. Great bosses and employees often reverse the typical job search: instead of the employee doing the "hunting," it's the boss. The process more resembles a "talent search" than a "job market."

5. While many gifted bosses have created such special work environments that they have virtually no turnover, many others embrace substantial turnover and become masters of "the secret skill" of firing.

6. An alliance between a gifted boss and a great employee is a kinship of talent, often creating a bond that can last a lifetime.

The Gifted Boss

★ ★ ★ ★ ★

What a Fool I'd Been

★ ★ ★ ★ ★

We keep hearing the cliché "I never met a man who looked back upon his life and wished he had spent more time at the office." Okay. Terrific. But what are we supposed to do with that insight? When people look back on their lives, what *do* they wish they'd spent more time doing?

Those two little questions ended up changing my life. I decided I would seek out the oldest, wisest people I could find and ask them to reflect upon their lives. I soon learned an important lesson: It's impossible to get wise old people to talk about regrets. With wisdom comes acceptance. The wise blame no one but themselves, and then they forgive themselves. The examined life is a process of peeling away the layers of stupidity. It may be that the greatest wisdom of all is to say, "What a fool I was!" and then to laugh.

And that discovery is where my story begins, for I have gained the freedom to see what a fool I'd been for most of my career.

"Only Connect"

★ ★ ★ ★ ★

My "wisest/oldest" project eventually led me to telephone Max Elmore. I'd saved him for last. He's an eccentric old sage I'd first met at O'Hare Airport, the two of us stranded together by a freak May snowstorm. At the time, I was a disheartened young bureaucrat, feeling stifled and stymied—feelings intensified that night by being one of thousands of frustrated travelers trying to nap while slumped against the walls, using our carry-on bags as pillows. Unable to relax, I watched glumly as an old guy in plaid pants appointed himself social director for all the restless children in the terminal. Once he exhausted them, he sat beside me, and I responded grouchily to his questions about my life, pouring out my frustrations. Instead of leaving me there to sulk, he cajoled me, then educated me, and ended up changing my life—literally overnight.

During our hours of conversation Max taught me that you can't get to *better* without first getting to *different*. And he showed me how to delight in flukes and coincidences and other offerings of the angels of creativity. I learned a new motto that night: Experiments Never Fail. Within a few weeks I had established a reputation within my company as an innovator, and I'd gotten pulled into a stream of new projects and eventually into a series of promotions. In fact, the success that followed my night with Max had led directly to the conundrum I now faced: I had more career than I wanted.

So it was fitting that I put off calling Max till the end, counting on him to help me pull together what I'd heard. And when I had him on the phone, I told Max that the more I searched, the more lost I had become.

He responded by asking, "So now that you've talked to all these wise old people, what do you think you should do more of?"

"Truly live. Experience life."

"Good. But what's the main ingredient of those experiences?"

"Other people."

"Yes. The goal isn't just to experience life, but to experience it together. Remember E. M. Forster? 'Only connect.' That's a two-word philosophy of life."

Those two words did indeed strike me as an important truth. But I was knee-deep in important truths. I said to Max, "I've been going in circles, reflecting on life. And since my life is mostly spent working, I've spent a lot of time reflecting on my career." I paused here, knowing I was about to say something that chilled me to contemplate, and I had to make sure my voice would not betray the powerful emotions I was feeling: "I've found myself wondering if I should quit my job, maybe become a consultant. Spend more time with my family."

There was a pause, and I couldn't decide if I would be pleased or disappointed if he agreed. Mine was an enviable job. Solid people, my coworkers. Good salary and benefits. Then again, I found myself not wanting to go to work some mornings, so much so that when the company started a little TGIM campaign, like we should all be thrilled to see Monday morning come around, I had to bite my tongue like it was a piece of Juicy Fruit.

Max finally responded by saying, "I remember hearing John Madden, the football coach, talking about his decision to become a television announcer. It happened not too long after he left coaching. He said something like, 'I quit coaching to spend more time with my family. But after a while, I realized that my family didn't want to spend more time with me. So I went back to work.'"

Max laughed, adding, "I'm picturing you quitting your job, and after a year or so, you discover that your wife and children are sneaking around, hiding from you." He feigned a child's high voice, "Shhh... get down. Here comes Dad again, trying to spend time with us."

We laughed together. Max knew me well enough to know that I already had a close family. Looking back, I suspect he understood that I was simply worn down and looking for an exit. I remarked, "So now I'm more confused than ever."

He said kindly, "I don't think the answer is 'not working.' The answer is carrying 'only connect' into your work. Business at its best is all about human involvement. The problem is that we've stripped work of its natural zest. I thought the old command structures were breaking down, but mostly it's been a sham. We talk about teams and coaches, but usually they turn out to be committees and managers working under aliases."

He was right about the company where I worked. I had left corporate life and built a small business of my own, then sold out to a larger company. Now I was a "team leader," which meant I was head of a small division. I had a couple of dozen people who worked for my group.

"So," Max said, "do you truly 'connect' with your bosses?"

"Sort of," I replied, knowing I sounded wishy-washy. They were bright, committed people, but it seemed I spent half my time trying to figure out how to get around their bureaucracy.

"Do you love them?"

"I wouldn't have chosen that word."

"Do you want to be more like them?"

"No."

"And how about the people who report to you? Do you 'only connect'?"

"I care about them."

"Not good enough. You undoubtedly 'care' about saving the whales. That's not the same as connecting."

I got a bit defensive here, because I am a good boss who has devoted himself to his division. So I threw out some objections while Max let me talk myself into a corner. Then, when I'd been "set up," Max took me into a brief conversation that changed forever the way I view work relationships.

"Have you ever had a *great* boss?" Max asked. "Someone you looked forward to seeing, who lifted you up to a higher plane?" I hesitated, debating one possibility in my mind. That's when he added, "Peter Schutz, the former CEO of Porsche, once described for me the type of relationship I'm talking about. He described it as 'I like *me* best when I'm around *you*.'"

With that I knew my answer—I'd never had a boss like that. And then he asked about my own management. I unburdened myself, explaining that my relationship with my employees was mostly as a problem solver. I spent my days with them lined up waiting to see me, and they invariably brought in their obstacles and screwups. I came through for them, and in doing so, I had stopped doing what I thought of as "actual work"—which I was good at, and enjoyed—and started being a corporate plumber, my life concerned with leaking projects and clogged pipelines.

Max started laughing as I finished my griping. "What?" I demanded. He responded, still amusing himself, "I just thought of a remark by Emperor Hirohito, commenting on how his life had changed after the war. He said, 'You can't imagine the extra work I had when I was a god.'"

He waited for me to laugh, but I merely forced a chuckle because I didn't find much humor or any applicability. He said, "Don't you see, you're trying to be the god of your department. It's a lousy job, being a god."

And then he asked me about the people who worked for me, and he wondered if I had any "great employees," whom he defined as people who not only needed no management but who also made me do better work, and who raised the entire department to a higher standard. So I had to say no, although I felt myself a bit of a traitor to say it. And then we got to the real goods....

The Best Place for the Best People

✫ ✫ ✫ ✫ ✫

So tell me your philosophy of hiring," Max said.

I didn't have one, of course, other than believing that I was a good manager and could get good performances from the competent people that Human Resources sent over. After some conversation, he summed up my hiring in a startling way:

"Let me get this straight. You hire from the candidates that HR sends over. And HR runs ads or gets unsolicited résumés in the mail and puts them in some sort of database. If you were a college basketball coach, these are what would be known as 'walk-ons'—people who just showed up and tried out. Which means that you and a team made up of 'walk-ons' are playing against teams that have searched the world for special talent."

This didn't sound like a terribly good strategy on my part. So I added something about networking (meaning the one employee I had hired after meeting her at a professional group).

"Okay," Max said. "But what do you do to make yourself attractive to great employees?"

I explained that our company offered "competitive wages and benefits" and that we had a "professional environment."

At this he snorted "No, no, NO!" so loudly that I had to

hold the phone out, away from my ear. "Listen to yourself. Think about those words. Those are dangerous phrases. When you say 'competitive wages' what you are saying is 'ordinary, average, about like everyone else's.' And when you say a 'professional environment' you are saying the same thing. 'Professional' means that it's typical of the profession, which is another way of saying that it's what's common, standard.' So you have, in effect, told me that your policy is to offer average rewards in an average environment. In other words, you are trumpeting your mediocrity."

This didn't sound right, but I knew it was true all the same. That's when he said, "What you want are the Wild Brains, the original thinkers, the self-reliants. They are the ones who lift up their coworkers and even their bosses. They set new standards. And they are *not* walk-ons. They rarely look for work. Only a moron of a boss lets one get away, although thank goodness there are such morons. But mostly you have to go to where the Wild Brains roam and coax them into following you home. And you can't coax extraordinary people with ordinary claims.

"Here's a little sentence that I use. Consider it a nine-word employment policy:

"The best place for the best people to work."

There was no mistaking the power of that statement, and I could immediately see how it would change almost everything about our work environment. Then again, it would never apply where I worked, not with the ax man continually cutting our budgets. I said simply, "I wish I could afford the best, much less the great employees with their Wild Brains."

He responded, "Once you understand what it is that great employees want, you'll see that it doesn't have to be expensive to hire the best people. In fact, all of my experience suggests that the best employees are a bargain."

Max paused, but I said nothing, not certain I believed in such magic employees, bargain or not.

I was glad to hear him say, "I can hear your eloquent silence, and it tells me that we have much to discuss, my friend." And then he made an offer that I jumped at: "If you want to learn how to be a great boss, worthy of great employees, and also learn how to be a great employee, worthy of a great boss, we need to get together and talk. We need a day—twenty-four hours. How about"—I heard him flipping a calendar—"oh, this could be perfect . . . there's something I want you to witness. A week from today in Phoenix?"

And that's how it was that I came to fly to Arizona to rendezvous with the eccentric business genius Max Elmore.

Sky Harbor

★ ★ ★ ★ ★

Max's instructions were for me to meet him at Sky Harbor Airport, in the oldest terminal, under a statue of a phoenix bird rising.

Finding Max is never difficult. As I hustled down the corridor, my plane late, I spotted his plaid pants at a hundred yards. As I came closer, I could see his gray hair combed straight back and his bolo tie—black strings below some sort of turquoise-in-silver piece. Being Max, he was entertaining strangers with some story. He was trying to remember a book title, and as I approached I could hear his self-deprecation: "I have a photographic memory—unfortunately it stopped offering same-day service." He laughed loudest of all. That was pure Max: He lived full volume, despite being in his seventies and having known the success that would have judged his silence as profundity.

When he spotted me, he roared a greeting and grabbed me up in a hug, slapping my back and barking profanities.

Then, pointing above his head, he asked how I liked the statue they'd done in honor of me and my career. It was a giant, gaudy phoenix, and naturally it was rising from the flames/ashes.

After retrieving my bag, we went to where he had parked a

rented Chevrolet Malibu in a yellow-striped zone designated for Truck Loading and Unloading. He'd left the trunk open, which, he explained, was enough to convince Security he qualified.

He said he was staying in the house of a friend, and I would be too. The friend and his wife were away in New York, so we'd have it to ourselves. It turned out to be south of South Mountain, on a street of Santa Fe–style houses that backed up to the rocky hills. He pulled into the drive of a long low house of pink stucco. Inside were Spanish tile floors and wildly colorful paintings.

It was a jewel of an October day—warm sun, cool breeze— and Max suggested that I settle down in one of the chocolate brown wrought-iron chairs on a back patio. There was no fence, just a low wall, and beyond that was an expanse of desert sloping to the rock cliffs. There were hundreds of those tall cactuses with arms, the saguaros, and a startling stillness that suggested that time had come here to rest. It was easy to picture Geronimo and his warriors riding their horses over this land.

My reflections were interrupted by the sound of a pop-top can being popped. Max handed me a Pepsi and said, "We have an appointment this afternoon." He sat across from me and began. "But before we go, here is our objective: I want your employers to be *crazy* about you. I want them to lie awake at night and thank the Lord that you work for them, and then lie there worrying that you might leave. I want them tossing around, trying to think of ways they can make you happier. Okay so far?"

Naturally I thought this was a solid objective, although I wanted to tell Max that it wasn't going to happen, not where I worked.

He said, "But because you are in the middle of the organization, not only do you want to be a great employee, you need to be a great boss. I'm going to show you how to turn your division into what I call a 'magnetic workplace.' I want all the best employees—the Wild Brains—to hear of your work and dream of being a part of it. Okay?"

I could only laugh and say, "Check. My bosses lying awake thanking God for me. The best potential employees dreaming of working for me. Everybody in bed, accounted for."

He leaned across from his chair to cuff me on the shoulder: "I'd forgotten what a smart-ass you are. Now I remember why I liked you."

Then Max announced that we would begin with a discussion of just what it is to be a "great boss" or "great employee." He began with a vocabulary switch. He said, "I'm going to refer to these great bosses as 'gifted bosses.' It will make sense as we go along." And then he offered the first revelation of the day.

The Gifted Boss
and the Great Employee

★ ☆ ★ ☆ ★

It turns out," Max began, "that both gifted bosses and great employees want the same thing from a workplace." He opened a leather portfolio that I hadn't noticed and pulled out a page of paper. "I prepared worksheets," he said, as though it were a natural thing for an eccentric old genius to do on behalf of a confused corporate bureaucrat.

The first page contained this:

> 1. The "talent-squared" workplace is possible because gifted bosses and great employees want the same things from a workplace:
>   - Freedom from . . .
>   management,
>   mediocrity and
>   morons.
>   - A change.
>   - A chance.

This list befuddled me, starting with the "talent-squared" business, but before I could start in with questions, Max explained: "When I began asking about great bosses, I soon learned that a major proportion of talented people—perhaps one out of three—have never had what they believed was a 'great' boss. Very few people have had more than one. But when I found those who'd had the experience, I asked how the boss had differed from the ordinary. The first and most passionate response was nearly always something to do with freedom—

"'He trusted me.'
"'He insulated us from the bureaucracy.'
"'She never got in the way and didn't let anybody else get in the way, either.'

"Then, in the next phase, when I asked the best bosses to describe the best employees, their first response category was *identical to that of the employees:* freedom. In the case of bosses, it was freedom from having to watch over an employee, from having to supervise and admonish.

"'She knew more about what needed to be done than I did—she'd tell me what to look for.'
"'I never have to worry about his work—he has higher standards than I do.'

"In other words, the gifted boss and great employee save each other from the agonies of management. And that's what I meant when I quoted on the phone that line from the late Emperor Hirohito, 'You can't imagine the extra work I had when I was a god.' The best bosses know how he felt: They have given up the role of knowing all, controlling all. When great bosses and great employees join together, many of the traditional functions of managing—giving assignments, supervising the work, checking up—become irrelevant. Supervision is replaced by trust, and trust requires no paperwork."

Max paused after that speech and let his eyebrows dance about, questioning.

"I'm with you," I said, "although I can't imagine employees who don't need any management. My biggest problem at work is that I can't do any real work, since I spend all my time helping the employees."

Max shook his head, saying, "That's the fundamental problem with management. Let's do a bit more figuring."

He took a legal pad, one with pink paper instead of the usual yellow, and wrote a large "10." He said, "This is the number of hours some guy in a corporation works—ten a day. And naturally, this person wants to get some help. So he convinces management to let him hire an assistant. Now the guy is a manager, and he cuts back to eight hours a day, the same as his new assistant."

Max wrote:

Manager: 10 − 2 = 8
Assistant: 8

"Now, say the manager spends two hours a day training, helping and supervising the assistant. Of course, the assistant also spends those same two hours being managed."

He changed the numbers on the legal pad.

Manager: 10 − 2 = 8   Then, 8 − 2 = 6
Assistant: 8 − 2 = 6

"So you add up the two new totals and what do you get? Twelve. And then you look where we started, and it was ten. So the corporation went from ten hours of work a day to twelve hours a day. But it costs the company nearly double. No wonder organizations are reluctant to add headquarters staff. And no wonder that individual managers think hiring is a great idea. That creates a natural tension in an organization."

He reached over and poked my knee for emphasis as he added, "And what if the boss spends another hour a day in managing, plus half an hour in conversation? Adding a new employee would actually reduce the number of hours worked per day." The poke turned into a squeeze. "That's why the gifted boss is engaged in a lifelong war with bureaucracy."

He sat back and said, "And the 'spoils of victory' in that war are the chances to put gifted bosses and great employees together and get what I call the 'talent-squared' effect. Both sides are freed from the drudgery of managing. Instead, each side inspires the other. True synergy. When you hire a great employee, suddenly you have lots of ideas about becoming more efficient, and soon you are each turning out more than either one of you could alone."

I nodded, trying to match his enthusiasm, although I had plenty of doubts. He read my mind and said, "Picture a five-person department, and you take the weakest employee away and add instead someone who is incredibly productive and creative, someone who not only turns out lots of work, but who also lifts the standards of the other employees, and who comes up with better ways to do the work. That one great employee can double the output of the entire department."

Then Max gave a finger-pointing, air-jabbing conclusion, "But ... but ... that will only happen if you're a gifted boss, secure enough to accept and to inspire greatness."

The Ordinary Boss

Versus

the Gifted One

★ ★ ★ ★ ★

Max leaned back to enjoy the breeze and watch the lizards chase one another along the wall. When he began anew he asserted, "The fundamental task of the best manager is not to manage." He looked hard at me. "Did you catch that one?" And then he repeated the business about the manager not managing. He continued: "The job of the gifted boss is to create a magnetic environment, one capable of attracting great employees—the kind who don't need management, who lift up their coworkers and even their boss. Agreed?"

I was still skeptical that such miracle employees existed, but I consented that it would be an ideal state.

"I can see you're not sold," he said, leaning back to give me a William F. Buckley Jr. dubious look, making me feel found out. "But you think that way," he said, "because Wild Brains don't come around very often. They don't go out looking for jobs. You have to believe in them in order to see them. Like fairies." This amused him so much that he brayed that whole-body laugh of his, which started him coughing.

He recovered soon enough and explained that he'd made a

list of a few of the differences between typical bosses and extraordinary ones. He handed me the list and let me read it over.

Looking at the list of traits of exceptional bosses, I said I could understand why Max had chosen the word *gifted* to describe the best bosses. Max responded, "When we turn to employees, you'll see that it would be easy to justify the same label for them. Both require skills that usually come with the IQ/EQ/AQ package that we drag along when we enter the workplace." He then said, mostly to himself, "Or does it drag us along?"

He shook his head, as if to shake away the distracting thought, then continued: "Back to the point. I've written down the qualities that seem to me to define the great bosses, who, in order to undertake even half of the items on the list, must have an exceptional energy level, plus a 'feel' for people that approaches the clairvoyant and/or charismatic. So 'gifted bosses' it is. And if you care to add that label to the best employees, you won't get an argument from me."

And with that he started in on the list of traits, beginning with one that seemed designed to tweak me.

> *The ordinary boss: offers good jobs, at competitive wages/benefits.*
> *The gifted boss: offers an exceptional environment, including the opportunity to be exceptional. Knows that his/her employees are in constant demand and so sets out to create a workplace that is magnetic.*

"Most companies are imitations," Max said, returning to a theme I'd heard at O'Hare Airport the evening we'd met. "They start small and imitate the ways of the giants in their field. This means that workplaces resemble one another. And when a company has an employment strategy like yours"—he paused long enough to put on a face and tone of great condescension—"of 'competitive' wages and benefits, it has put up the flag of mediocrity."

He leaned in to press the point: "I suppose that every manager looks in the mirror and believes that a leader is looking back, but in that reflection is usually just a bureaucrat with embossed business cards."

I realized at that minute that I did take pride in my business cards. After all, once you reached the "senior" level at our corporation, you got the more expensive cards—not just embossed, but color.

He continued: "First, the gifted boss envisions and creates an environment that people want to be part of. You find major programs like"—he repeatedly snapped his fingers into a bunch, as if to literally pull recollections out of the air—"3M's '15% Rule'—where employees are encouraged to devote 15 percent of their work time to pet projects of their own choosing. That's the sort of program that announces to the world, THIS IS NO ORDINARY WORKPLACE." He said the last phrase in a booming orator's voice.

"But," he said, poking the air, "the same announcement is often made in smaller, less serious ways as well. For instance, the CEO at China Mist Tea, Dan Schweiker, replaced the table in the conference room with a pool table. That may sound like a trifle, but it's important as a cultural statement. Just like when Dan got rid of the reserved parking spaces for executives. And beyond such symbolic changes, there is a different feeling—the air seems different, the people bounce. One of Dan's employees said to me, "After many years in a stuffy, driven environment, this new job is almost like being on vacation."

Max stopped to scrutinize my reaction. Not satisfied, he added: "Or take Insight—it's a thriving computer retailer that we're going to visit tomorrow morning. It was founded by two brothers who even now are only in their thirties. When one of them, Eric Crown, was helping design the new headquarters building, he had it built in the shape of a giant X. He wanted the different departments to pass in the halls, to figuratively, if not literally, bump into one another. And instead of 'dress-down Fridays,' they created what they called 'dress-up Mondays,' having one day a week when employees can choose to take off the casual wear and put on traditional business attire. And they've subcontracted with two firms that work with the handicapped to staff one of their departments. You should see these folks in action. They are delighted to be working. And they lift the whole organization with their everyday courage. It's hard to be depressed over the cold sore on your lower lip when the person working down the hall struggles to walk."

He pressed on: "Or there's the example of a company called Tires Plus, a chain of tire shops. At their headquarters, they have not only a fitness room but also a massage room and a *meditation room*. They are in the tire business, but they have a meditation room . . . can you imagine?"

Max was clearly enthralled with these stories, but I was still doubtful. He tested my reserve with a touching story about a worldwide project undertaken by Lenscrafters. They set a goal to donate a million eye exams to impoverished people around the world. Employees compete for the privilege of taking part, earning a trip to a Third World country to do eye tests and pass out eyeglasses. With that as background, Max told me of the time he met the company's CEO, Dave Browne, who told him of his own experience with the program:

"Browne joined a group of employees spending a week
in rural Mexico. Because he had no experience at the
actual measuring and adjusting, he was assigned to setting

up and cleaning up. Then, after days of observing and helping, he got his chance to actually fit glasses. It was going well, villager after villager, when up came a young woman who was legally blind. At twenty years of age, she had literally seen almost nothing of the world. Her vision reached a few blurry inches, and she made her living doing needlepoint, spending her days with the material and thread virtually touching her nose as she squinted to do her patterns.

"Browne found the strongest pair of glasses they had, and as he slipped them onto her face, she grabbed at them, falling to the ground, shrieking. He could only think that he had stuck her in the eye and knelt beside her wondering, Oh Lord, what have I done to this poor girl? As he tried to comfort her, an interpreter heard her screams and rushed over, only to smile down at Dave Browne and the weeping young woman. 'She's saying that it's a miracle, that she can see, that she has been touched by the hand of God.' Touched by the hand of God. That is a kind of miracle, isn't it? Wouldn't that change the way you think of work?"

I was moved by the story and said so. But I had to add that all these efforts struck me as "nice," but not "decision criteria" for choosing where to work. When I voiced my doubts, Max flopped back in his seat, acting offended. He said, "That's the rut you're in and you don't even know you're in it. It's a glass rut. It's funneling you along and you don't even see it."

I smiled at the image.

"Yes, A...GLASS...RUT!" He said the words loudly, leaning forward to slap the table for emphasis, causing the cans to shudder. Max didn't notice because he had realized the time and was standing up. He said, "Enough talk. It's time to go visit a magnetic workplace."

And so we were back in the car, headed for downtown Phoenix. "I have to tell you about John Genzale," Max said as we headed up Central Avenue. Just that name sent Max chuckling. "His employees call him the Lion and bring him all sorts of lion crap—stuffed animals and posters, that sort of thing. I love to tease him about it. That's who we're going to meet."

We eventually stopped at a low building among the highrises, the offices of the *Phoenix Business Journal.* We came into the reception area but got no reception—it was deserted. Although just four-thirty, it appeared that work for the day had ended earlier. Max continued on toward a room in the back, waving for me to follow. We slipped in quietly and there found twenty or so employees, some in chairs, others on the floor, all intent on a man who was reading poetry. "That's him," Max whispered. "Our lion."

Well, he paced in a leonine way—loose jointed and self-assured—but more closely resembled a television news anchor—he wore an expensive suit coat, a quiet but assertive tie in a perfect knot, and the shirt had French cuffs with gold cuff links.

That first poem was by Tennyson, I learned later. One passage ended with a line that seemed particularly appropriate:

"Some work of noble note, may yet be done.
Not unbecoming men that strove with gods.
The lights begin to twinkle from the rocks:
The long day wanes: the slow moon climbs: the deep
Moans round with many voices. Come, my friends,
'Tis not too late to seek a newer world."

The Tennyson reading went on for a while, followed by a discussion of the images and the wordings. But it wasn't all serious, there was joking fun too, like a scene from the movie *Dead Poets Society*. And then Genzale took up a book of love poems, saying that it had been brought in by one of the employees named Steve. This was deemed to be funny by the audience. I guess you had to know Steve.

The reading and chatting went on for half an hour, with no one showing anything less than complete attention. After the employees had headed home, Max and Genzale embraced and reminisced and then got around to discussing what I'd just seen. Genzale explained: "We're a weekly business paper. It's not what most of us went to journalism school to do. And we don't have the resources of a big daily paper. But that doesn't mean we can't grow and develop as writers, that we can't set a standard for passionate writing. So I started weekly poetry readings in the newsroom. And what happened was that we got everyone reading poetry, which got everyone thinking about fine writing."

Max put his arm around Genzale and added, "Forget about what that says to the world, think about what current employees can say to potential employees: Hey, where we work, we're evolving as writers... we even have poetry readings."

Max beamed at me, and I said truthfully that I was impressed—not just that the group had found something to be passionate about, but that they all had committed the time to be passionate together. That's when Max told me that I needed to "find my poetry." He added, "What we're really talking about is 'niche marketing.' You have to think of yourself as marketing your department to the company, and also as marketing your department to prospective employees. You identify that one trait that you want associated with your department, and then you find a way to evolve that strength. That second part is important: Too often a manager or a company president will declare a 'vision' or a 'mission' and then do nothing to support it. It's one thing to declare that you're going to be innovative; it's another to find ways to evolve creativity, to get everyone thinking creatively.

Genzale offered an example to support Max's point: "There's an ad agency with offices here in Phoenix and in Atlanta called After Dark. As a reward for meeting their annual goals, they all went to Paris. They did the trip right too. For small money you could bring your spouse or a friend. And it wasn't 'mandatory fun' where they had a lot of planned events. They split up, explored on their own. But what they did during the trip, and after, was to talk about all the design elements they had seen. They immersed themselves in beauty. Now they're planning their next trip—Italy."

We talked a while longer before leaving the newspaper. After we got back in the car, I told Max that the poetry reading idea suggested some things I could do with my department . . . or part of it at least. I told Max, "I could apply that to the professional group. But more than half the people who work for me are clerical or technical. I feel sorry for those people. I have to tell you, those are dull jobs."

Max didn't hesitate. He responded with this story:

"Take the case of Maggie Lifland, who built three insurance agencies in resort towns in Colorado. She started out with the typical assembly line approach, where you break jobs down till they are simple enough for anyone to do. Even the smallest mind grows bored. So the structure ensures turnover and discontent, and thus you enter a downward spiral where the jobs get ever simpler as you have to constantly replace the people doing them. But, as

Lifland put it, *'If you're a manager and you create jobs that are so boring that you wouldn't want to do them, why should your employees?'*

"She observed that the employees were isolated and sedentary, and that the employees highly valued the activities outside the office—after all, they were in resort towns in Colorado.

"The existing setup for the insurance offices was for each person to have a set of accounts and to handle everything to do with them. Lifland decided to centralize the files so the employees shared clients and could cover for one another. And once everyone shared work, the company was able to institute a four-day work week, three weeks of vacation per year, and an environment where 'day-swapping' is encouraged. And the company also started quarterly growth bonuses that are split equally.

"The agencies saw an immediate drop in turnover and, over time, the ability to attract highly talented employees, the sort who can be choosy about a workplace. All it took to begin was one question: If I wouldn't want to do the job, why should they? A leader doesn't just share the profits, but the wealths—the joy and satisfaction and flexibility and freedom of *ownership*. And these new jobs give an employer a story to use to romance great employees."

"But," I said, enjoying the chance to ask what seemed to me a tough question, "it's *still* pretty dull work."

He gave a hard grimace. "Okay, you're right. Some jobs are just jobs. Of course, there are plenty of people who just want to leave work at work and don't seem to mind 'dull' so much. In fact, there's a guy named Ron Healey—nothing dull about him— who's a consultant with a program called 30/40, where manufacturing firms replace a forty-hour week with thirty hours while pay stays the same. The employees come in for a six-hour shift and work straight through. Output goes up, as does the number and quality of job applicants. Turnover, absences and mistakes go down."

"Six hours straight?" I moaned in sympathy for those employees. "I'm not sure that's an improvement."

"The logic is that employees are only really productive about six hours a day, no matter how many hours they are there, so why not let them put in those hours and leave. As Healey puts it, 'We give people their lives back.' And he also is willing to admit that a lot of the jobs are just monotonous chores, being assistants to machines. He's stopped trying to pretend that they can be made deeply rewarding. Instead, they let people have time to do other things. He had one employee say, '*I don't have a great job, but I have a great life.*'"

Max concluded by saying, "Notice that the NO ORDINARY WORKPLACE sign is lit. There's a waiting list to get on at those companies, despite the type of work and the labor shortages at competitors."

Max smiled as he continued driving along Central Avenue, through downtown. "Now, you're ready for a story that you won't believe. Dave Thomas—you know, Wendy's hamburgers— told me that he didn't have a business plan when he started the company and still doesn't have one. Instead, he had a simple dream: to own his own restaurant, and maybe if things went well, to own three or four around town."

He saw me looking underwhelmed. "No, that's not the 'hard

to believe' part. What's hard to believe is that when he started the first Wendy's, it was after he'd spent years as a gifted boss while working at Kentucky Fried Chicken. Thomas knew so many great employees that he didn't have room for all of them. And he began to expand for the sake of the employees, trying to fit them all in. He explained it to me: 'I had people who I'd worked with before who wanted to work for me. I'd tell them, 'I can't pay you very much.' They'd say, 'That doesn't make any difference.' So I had to open up more stores. When you have people who are with you, and believe in you, you have a responsibility to them.' "

Max again saw my skepticism and said, "I know it sounds implausible but sitting with him, I believed it. And I've felt it in my own business life. When you know a great employee, it starts you dreaming: What could we do together?

"The fellow I mentioned to you before, the one with the tea company, Dan Schweiker, told me that for years he had done all the selling for the company. He and his partner had been considering hiring some salespeople but decided to wait another year. Then right after they had made that decision, two competitors' salespeople called him and said they wanted to work there. Two. From different companies. On the same day. And he took that as a sign that maybe he should let go of some of the selling. So he hired them both and told them, 'I'm not going to try to tell you what to do. We're hiring you to learn from you.' That was one of the great leaps forward in the history of the company."

Max stopped and inhaled. "I get so excited talking about all this that I almost forget to breathe," he said. "See what I mean about 'magnetic'? Your competitors' best people coming to you. And you can even turn your customers into headhunters. Suzanne Mollerud, who runs a chain of hair salons in Minnesota called Kids' Hair, told me how one of her best stylists came to work there. The stylist called and said, 'One of my customers has been telling me about what a great atmosphere you have at your salons.' "

And he inclined his head to me as he said, "That's ..." and waited for me to finish. I wasn't sure if he was looking for No Ordinary Workplace or the Magnetic Workplace, so I mentioned both.

Then he circled right back to finish up a point. "And don't forget that part about Thomas saying, 'I can't pay you very much.' There's the magic of a gifted boss. Some companies pay exceptional wages in order to attract top performers—in the words of one executive, 'I don't know how to motivate employees, but I know how to bribe them.' But once employees have experienced a gifted boss, they know that they'll get something more important than a starting salary—a chance and a change. Knowing the gifted boss, they know they'll get opportunities, and trust that income will follow."

Max's Magnetic Workplace was interesting, in an academic way. After all, I was in the midst of a large corporation, tightly controlled by the management structure and by the Human Resources department. "It's a beautiful dream," I told him. "And maybe I should get out of corporate life and start up my own company again. But till I do, I don't see it happening."

Loving nothing more than a challenge, Max made a face and then told me to get out the list of traits. At the next stoplight he leaned over to point at the sheet I held, saying, "Let's jump ahead to this one. Yes, this is it. The example I have for this one comes from a man who was in the military. You think you don't have much latitude ... HA!" And then he sat back to let me read the following.

The ordinary boss: has clear rules and ethics.

The gifted boss: has few rules but high standards. (The best one-sentence summary of good management I've ever heard: "Be big about the petty stuff and be petty about the big stuff.")

"Listen to the story of John Welker," Max said, wagging his head in a show of cockiness. "He's now a stockbroker with Merrill Lynch, but he had this realization during his days in the army. He was given the assignment of heading an artillery battalion stationed in Germany. Soon after arriving, he decided to test his troops by simulating an attack. In other words, a situation where the guns needed to be set up as quickly as possible.

"He issued the order to prepare to fire, then stood and watched. Then stood and watched some more. His troops put on a bumbling display of incompetence. After half an hour, he walked away, his troops still struggling. It was *The Three Stooges Go to War*. A joke."

Although I'd never been in the military, I'd had enough employees to relate.

"So," Max continued, "what to do? Yell? Study procedure manuals? The next morning Welker called a veteran artillery officer and asked, 'How long should it take to set up guns?' The answer: 'About nine minutes.' And that morning Welker went to his troops and announced that they should figure out how to get the guns ready to fire in eight minutes. He didn't tell them how to do it—he established a standard and let them work it out. And a few days later, one of them came to him, trying not to smile, and said, 'Sir, we're ready for you to time us.' And of course they beat the time easily. That experience inspired Welker to replace a two-hundred-page procedure manual with a one-page list of standards. And within a year, his battalion was named the best of its type in the world."

Knowing he had gotten to me with that story, Max grinned and added, "Did you catch that? The best in the world. That incident changed Welker's life. He gave up on policy manuals in favor of standards—not rules, but definitions of excellence."

I liked the story and knew I could learn from it. But I told Max that I wasn't clear on the difference between a rule and a standard. And I also remembered how Max liked to belittle the whole planning and goal-setting process. So, just to provoke him, I told him it sounded like "goal setting" to me.

He did a long lip-farting exhalation. "Okay, it may seem like mere semantics—rules, goals, standards . . . same difference. No. *Rule* comes from the Latin *regula* for *rod*, as in a ruler. Rules are part of formal procedure, the currency of bureaucracy, and are, of course, 'made to be broken.' As for *goals*, the origin is unknown, presumed to be derived from some forgotten sport. It suggests a 'line' to cross, a possibility.

"Now, my young and I must say *cynical* friend, compare those two words to *standard*, which is not just a 'benchmark' but an 'upright support,' as in construction and as in a flagpole. *Standard* has two possible origins—the Frankish word, *standard*—that is, 'stand hard,' or Old French *estandard*—that is, 'rallying place.'

"A standard can shape a company and its employees. When I did some work for Procter & Gamble, the staff told me proudly of the company's standard for entering a new household product category: P & G's product would be introduced only if it could beat the existing category leader in a consumer test using unlabeled products. That simple statement shaped the entire company. It told the folks in R & D not to waste their time on "me-too" products. It told the sales force that their time wouldn't be wasted hawking mediocrity. It eliminated countless debates and meetings. And it imbued the organization with a world-beater attitude.

"And that is the beauty of a standard. It *stands up* and proclaims: Here's what we *stand for*, the ground we *stand upon*; here's how we *stand apart* and *stand out*; and this is where we *stand together*."

Here he paused to give my knee another of his iron grips. He said with some emotion, "One standard is worth a thousand committee meeting."

He pointed to the sheet of traits that I still held and instructed me to write in a new one:

> *The ordinary boss: understands how to function within the*
> *bureaucracy.*
> *The gifted boss: knows how to work outside the bureaucracy.*

And after writing, he added, "Now, does your employer have more restrictions than the U.S. Army?"

"I think not."

"And could you not adopt standards for your division?"

"I already have some in mind."

At that he slapped me on the shoulder. "Now, that's my boy!"

Trying to join in with his mood, I said, "Just because I work in a bureaucracy doesn't mean I have to think like a bureaucrat."

"What you have to do is to think like an antibureaucrat. It's that glass rut I was talking about earlier. Your mind is being conditioned to think just like everyone else's around you. Nothing sinister about it, that's just the way it works. And so if you want to distinguish yourself, you have to make a conscious effort to do so. Just like you have to make a conscious effort to create a unique workplace."

Here we were, venturing into the lessons Max had taught me years before. I repeated back to him one of his favorite lines: "You can't get to 'better' without going through 'different.'"

He nodded. "By being a gifted boss you are going to create a workplace that sells great employees on the idea of working for you. And if you're going to sell, the best way to sell is via word of mouth. You need to give them something to talk about." And he sang, badly, some lines from the song "Something to Talk About." He got to the part where it goes, "How about love?" And then he said, "That is our goal here. We are talking about love. Not about benefits or 401(K)s—we're talking about love."

He pulled into a parking garage for a large complex called the Arizona Center, saying, "I thought we'd eat here, but these old bones are getting tired of sitting. Let's go for a stroll first." He instructed me to take along the list.

It was late afternoon as we left the parking garage, the sun sharp between shadows. We walked along the downtown streets, past the Herberger Theater with its line of statues of frolicking nudes, past Symphony Hall.

As we walked, I read aloud from Max's list.

The ordinary boss: has answers.
The gifted boss: has questions. (Understands that letting employees
figure out the answers is more important than the answer
itself.)

This one seemed aimed at me. I said, "If you could show me how to stop being the department Answer Man, it would change my life overnight."

He laughed and said, "You're too easy. That one is . . ." And he snapped his fingers. "I learned that lesson from Peter Schutz, the former CEO of Porsche who I've told you about. I once complained to him that I was working too hard. He asked me how I spent my time, and I said 'Solving problems.' And he practically yelled at me, 'STOP DOING THAT!' I was falling into the same trap that you are now in. If people can come to you to get their problems solved, they'll just keep coming back. Why should they take the risk of solving problems? If you solve them, then you get the blame. And that's what most companies are about—avoiding blame."

This reminded me, I told Max, of an article I'd read that said the number one reason people say no to salespeople is the fear of making a mistake. And this had changed the way I sold my ideas to the company. I realized that while I was going on about the wonderful things we might accomplish with some new project, the executives were sitting there thinking only one thing: *What could go wrong?* So I'd learned to "inoculate" against fears by explaining how we could minimize any risk, especially the risk of management looking bad.

One of the things I'd learned from my previous conversations with Max was a motto that I used when presenting ideas: "People hate to change, but love to experiment." A change is a risk. An experiment is something you can undo, can walk away from wiser. So I'd learned to make new projects into experiments, usually with small pilot programs.

Max enjoyed hearing me feed back his insights and put his arm around me. I felt like a character in a movie, walking through the twilight with this sage beside me.

"Now," he said, squeezing my shoulder before turning loose, "you have explained your own solution. When employees bring you their questions, what are your experiments?"

"Turn the tables and ask them the questions."

"Exactly. You could run a department by asking two questions all day long, 'Is there a better way?' and 'Is this the best you can do?' The best employees will tell you how their work could be better. And they will love you for insisting they do it. Which takes us to the next of the traits."

The ordinary boss: buys employees' time and effort.
The gifted boss: buys help.

When I looked up, Max had started in on what seemed to me to be an irrelevant digression, but he soon proved me wrong.

"You know those little news items where they go out to a church and show some everyday item where the face of Jesus or the Virgin Mary has appeared?" I nodded, chuckling at the abrupt shift in subject.

"Well, a few months back I was watching one such report and found myself admiring the warmth and earnestness of those who had come to visit, especially as compared to the know-it-all newscasters who had come to scoff. And that's when this thought occurred to me: You will only spot the face of Jesus in a tortilla if you spend a lot of time thinking about Jesus. Your tortilla is a mirror of your mind."

This was such a silly image that I had to smile, but Max was in a dreamy state, adding, "I knew, of course, that I had merely reinvented the Rorschach test. But doing so, I rediscovered the importance of prevailing perceptions, and how we must take care as to what we allow ourselves to dwell upon. All of which leads to an interesting workplace question: What's in your organization's mind?"

My answer was going to be "How to get out of work." But Max had meant it to be rhetorical, and he provided his own answer: "Our corporations train their employees to think about the corporation, about rules, and, as you were saying a minute ago, about what can go wrong. In other words, we bathe ourselves in bureaucracy and then expect people not to act like bureaucrats.

"So," he continued, "the job of a great boss becomes to manage the corporate version of the 'collective unconscious.' I once fell into a conversation with a doctor who told me that he'd gone through fourteen assistants in one year. None seemed to live up to his standards of patient care. Finally, he went to a friend, a surgeon whose office he had visited, and said, 'You have the most wonderful staff here. How do you do it?' The surgeon said that the candidates go through three interviews, not just with him but with the other staff members. But all three interviews only screened out candidates, setting the stage for a single question that determined who got hired. That question is, 'What compassion do you have to offer my patients?'

"Using that question, the doctor solved his turnover problem. Why? Because he was able to hire people who understood pain, who understood illness, and who wanted to do something about it. It seems so simple, doesn't it? Imagine a medical office full of people who radiate compassion. And now compare that mental picture to the typical behind-the-glass, fill-out-the-forms medicrats."

Max continued: "Not every business wants to put compassion first, of course. But every organization could go in search of a related trait—the willingness to help. Shame that most newspapers have stopped calling the job ads the Help Wanted section. I know when I hire someone it's *help* that I want. It's much easier to get employees than to get help. There's an entire philosophy of business in that single word *help*. Here's a two-word employee handbook: *just help*. And how's this for a two-word mission statement: *we help*."

He turned to me and I nodded in agreement.

He continued: "It's easy to spot an organization bathed in bureaucracy versus one bathed in helping. For instance, there's a health club near where I live, one of those giant ones, with an acre of chrome torture equipment in back and a sales operation in the front. On the wall near the sales desks is a sign: PLEASE DON'T ASK TO USE THE PHONES. If you care about helping your customers, and they repeatedly asked to use the phone, you'd install a phone for customers to use, right? That's just what they've done at Blockbuster Video, at least the one near my home. There's a phone that encourages you to call home and discuss movie choices. That's helping your customers.

"All of which reminds me," Max said, "of Jay Goltz, a man who turned a frame shop in Chicago into a ten-million-dollar business. Goltz argues that 'there is always a better answer than just yes.' He gives the example of the guy who moves to a new city and is trying to find an auto repair shop to service his Lotus. He calls several and asks each of them if they work on Lotuses. A few say yes, but then one says, 'Absolutely, we specialize in imports, and the shop's owner drives a Lotus.' Ah, a better answer. Any good employee will answer a question, but only a few actually understand the customer and truly seek to help.

"That is a trait of a great employee, of course. But it's the job of a gifted boss to find such people and to create an environment in which everyone is thinking about helping."

He stopped then and turned to me: "So, what compassion do you bring along to work? What preoccupies the mind of your division? That's what will be waiting for you in your tortilla." And then he laughed that great laugh of his and started walking again.

✯ ✯ ✯ ✯ ✯

We walked on for another block, neither of us needing to talk. The air at dusk was somehow richer than usual and seemed worthy of taking in slowly and savoring. This serene mood was interrupted by Max saying, "Are we lost?"

"I don't think so. Isn't that next cross street the one that runs past the place where we're eating.'

He seemed a bit disappointed by this answer. I guessed that Max is the sort who enjoys being lost. He said, "Let's ask, just to be certain." And with that he wandered up to a sidewalk café and started talking to a tableful of businessmen. Max asked directions, but that merely started a conversation, and we ended up sitting in with them, sharing their pitcher of margaritas.

Refreshed by our break, we resumed our walk. The night air was cooler, but it still felt thick and welcoming. Passing under a streetlamp, I read the next trait out loud for Max.

The ordinary boss: allows you to keep growing.
The gifted boss: kicks you up to the next rung in your personal ladder
of evolution.

Max started by quoting a comedian named Brian Kiley: *"I went to a bookstore the other day. I asked the woman behind the counter where the self-help section was. She said, 'If I told you, that would defeat the whole purpose.' "*

"I love that line," Max continued, "because one of the distinguishing traits of the gifted boss—a trait that would justify by itself the use of the word *gifted*—is the 'feel' for bringing along an employee. Often an employee is hired not for current skills but for potential. The gifted boss is like a chess master, operating several moves in the future, sensing just when an employee can succeed at something new, often before the employee knows it." He had me stop at the next streetlamp to show me that he'd put several subheadings under this trait. Max gave an example to go with each one. Here's my best recollection of what he said:

MAKING PEOPLE UNCOMFORTABLE

"I talked with Angelo Petrilli," Max said, "when he was a vice president of one of the divisions of Bell Sports. He said of his employees, 'I find people with heart—you better hire it, because you sure can't put it in there.' And working for Petrilli is not for the faint of heart because he says, 'I believe in putting people in situations a little above their heads. Put them where they are uncomfortable. I'm not looking for maintenance people.' In fact, he takes comfort as his signal to introduce change. He said, 'For instance, I had an employee who gave a presentation to me. Marvelous. I told her, "Come with me and *you* present it to the CEO." She said, "I can't do that." And I told her, "It's not that you can't do it, you just don't know you *can* do it." Or, if I have staff people who get comfortable, I'll have them work directly with a client. They get comfortable with that, and I have them go along on sales calls. Later I might have them make some sales calls, ones where their expertise is a good match.'"

Max added, "What Petrilli wants is for his staff to be on a personal adventure as well as a corporate one. You've heard that expression 'wheels-within-wheels'; well, the gifted boss offers 'adventures-within-adventures.' The company or the department is experimenting, and within it, the boss is pushing the employees into their personal adventures. Earlier I said that you could manage with the question, 'Is that the best you can do?' Well, I guess we should modify that to include the possibility of not accepting the first yes. The great boss knows how to expect more than the employees expect of themselves."

PASSING THE BATON

"One trait of gifted bosses is letting go of authority. Indeed, they don't just let go of it, they shove it over to someone else. Nancy Loftin is the chief legal counsel for APS, a major utility company here in Arizona. Her predecessor was promoted to CFO, so he was still around and seemingly still available for legal opinions. Loftin told me, 'Not only had the other executives relied upon his advice for years, but it was quite a change for the company to have a woman in my position. Besides, he was a genius, and had a photographic memory. So it's not surprising that people still went to him with questions. But he wouldn't answer them. He'd just say, "I don't know—check with Nancy." He knew the answer—oh, he *knew*. Saying he didn't was his way of passing the baton.' "

As we waited for a streetlight, Max turned to me to say, "It sounds like an easy matter, to refer questions to the new person, but imagine the self-confidence it takes to say, 'I don't know,' and thus end any second-guessing. And speaking of self-confidence, the old boss built up Loftin's confidence with other quiet refusals. She would go to him to try to get him to intervene in tricky corporate matters, and he would say, 'You can handle it.' She said of those occasions, 'It sounds dismissive, but it wasn't. It was his vote of confidence. And I admired him so much that if he had confidence in me, I had to have confidence in me too.' "

WIN BY LOSING

As we continued walking, Max asked me if I was ready to have a real challenge to my own self-confidence. I said I didn't think so, which made him punch my shoulder. "In that case," he said, "put this one away for later. But you should know that the most daring way of challenging employees is simply by being wrong, by losing an argument to them."

Max told me he'd learned that principle from Ken Donahue, the president of a division of Teledyne, headquartered in Philadelphia. He explained as follows:

> "Ken said a remarkable thing: 'Sometimes I'll have an idea, and the employees will raise issues. And sometimes the facts are with the employees. And I change my mind, drop my sword, and support them. Once you do that, they know it's okay. If you ignore them, and bully through, they think, 'Why should I disagree and end up with emotional scars?' But if they see you admit you're wrong, they learn that it's worthwhile to challenge you. And if they see you change, they'll do it too.'
>
> "In other words, being wrong—and admitting it— becomes just another way the gifted boss develops and motivates great employees.
>
> "And all of this can lead to the possibility that an employee who doesn't start 'great' can be challenged to greatness by a skilled leader."

This took us to the last item on Max's list.

The ordinary boss: seeks team players.
The gifted boss: seeks allies.

"I propose," said Max, pointing to a restaurant, "that we delay the last item till after dinner. Once we talk about great employees, and the alliances they create with gifted bosses, you'll know what you have to do." He turned to me, and I nodded.

"So it's dinner and a discussion of what it takes to be a great employee—both so you can spot them, and so you can be one."

It felt odd to think of myself as an employee. As soon as I'd risen into management, I'd thought of myself as a manager, as a leader. I never gave any thought to what it took to be a better employee, a better follower. But I didn't have time to contemplate this because Max had stopped just outside the entrance to ask me, "So did anything we've talked about strike you as helpful, or have you just been humoring the old guy?"

"Max," I said earnestly, "yesterday I didn't even know it was there, but now I can feel that glass rut closing in on me. Without meaning to, I devoted all my leadership skills and creativity to accomplishing this: an above-average environment for average employees." Max applauded. "And now," I added over his clapping, "I'm determined to go back and create the best place for the best people to work."

The Ordinary Versus
the Great Employee

★ ★ ★ ★ ★

We ate dinner at Sam's Café, which is on the ground floor of the Arizona Center, one of those giant complexes of offices and retail. Max asked for a quiet spot, and we were seated off to one side of the outdoor dining, looking out on a tree arbor that seemed out of place but tranquil all the same.

When he got around to describing his research on bosses and employees, he told me that he had gone in search of gifted bosses, and then asked them what they looked for in their best employees. "So," he concluded, "my sample was only of gifted bosses. I'm not saying that these are the qualities that every boss craves—then again, who cares what the 'average boss' wants?—these are the traits you need if you are to attract the attention of a great boss. And, by the way, as we shall see in the next phase, that great bosses don't hire employees; they 'talent-hunt' those 'Wild Brains' I was telling you about."

I wanted to hear more about the "talent-hunting," but Max wouldn't be dissuaded: "No, no, no. You mustn't get in a hurry on this one. First, you must be great and then you shall be sought after. Which reminds me of a television executive, Grant Tinker, who had just taken over one of the networks and was asked how he planned to make his network number one. He said simply, 'First we will be best, and then we will be first.' Isn't that marvelous?"

I agreed. But I was eager to move on, so I asked Max, "So what does it take to be 'best' among employees?"

"First, there is the obvious quality—the great ones are exceptionally productive. Which doesn't necessarily mean they work the longest hours. They aren't always the coffee-makers, first one in, but they produce results."

"No surprise there."

"Exactly, and that's why I'm not going to waste a lot of time talking about it. Being a great employee isn't about 'grinding' as much as it is about 'soaring.' We've already said that a great boss and a great employee want the same things—one, freedom; two, a change; and three, a chance. And by defining the great bosses, we have already defined the great employee. In fact, one of the joys of an alliance between two talented people is that the status distinctions fall away, the two merge."

Max gave me a look, and said, "Well, I can see I'm boring you with philosophy—what you want are specifics. And specifics you'll get. First, let's talk about *freedom*—that is, the no-management employee."

Max turned earnest as he said, "The first freedom is trust, knowing that the work will get done and done at least as well as if you had done it yourself. Look at these comments." And he showed me the first list of remarks he had written down, quotes taken verbatim from gifted bosses describing their best employees.

The great ones never let themselves do second-rate work.

If you're in a bind, there they are, jumping in and helping. You don't even have to ask, *they just know*.

The best employees are their own worst critics—you never have to criticize them, only congratulate.

They dream your dream—you know they have the same agenda you do.

Great employees aren't like children—Did you make your bed? No, with great employees you know that *you are always being helped.*

With them, you don't have to watch your back—they're watching it for you.

Max continued: "The second freedom is handing over parts of your job. The great employees have at least one skill superior to the boss's, and/or serve as a check on the boss's work."

The best employees tap you on the shoulder and ask what you can hand off to them.

My best employee was everything I wasn't, and vice versa.

They tell me what we need, not me telling them.

Great employees have standards that lift us all up. We don't want to disappoint them.

The great ones have a real emotional investment with the customers and understand the customers better than anyone else in the organization.

"It takes a gifted boss to have employees like these, because they are themselves leaders. Other employees look to them and go to them. A boss can feel irrelevant, unless that boss is doing gifted work, creating the magnetic workplace. Agreed?"

I nodded, although inside I was shaking my head, thinking of how far my current employees were from these ideals.

"The next thing," Max said, "that great employees want, and that great bosses love to see, is *change*. They are *'what's next?'* people who are eager for morning. But they don't just sit back in the audience to change, they are onstage. Here are some of the comments I wrote down."

> The best employees seem to perform best in the midst of problems or chaos. They bring a calm to the group. Their self-confidence is contagious.

> The best ones "crystallize" information. They don't talk in technical lingo, they present the options.

> My best employees were the ones who would *show me the possibilities*.

Max tapped the page and said, "Don't you love that one about 'show me the possibilities?' It reminds me of that phrase from some movie: 'show me the money.'"

"Jerry Maguire."

"Yes. That's the one. And when an employee shows you the possibilities, it's the same thing. That comment came from John Genzale, our poetry reading lion. And after he said that about 'possibilities,' I remember he went on to compare a great employee to an architect who you hire to build your new warehouse. You specify a big box, but a good architect will come back and say, 'This is what you want me to do, but I could also do this...or this. The best will open you up."

I added, "When I read the ones about adversity, I thought of a quote you told me, one from Golda Meir: 'A new problem is as good as a vacation.'"

"Wouldn't it be great for you to do a role reversal on your staff. You were telling me how your employees line up outside your door, bringing you their problems. Imagine walking into the office of a great employee and saying, 'We've got a problem' and hearing, 'I'll take care of it. Don't worry.' And you wouldn't worry. It would be like those great P. G. Wodehouse novels, the ones where Bertie is always getting into a jam and running to his butler, Jeeves, for a solution. Jeeves is the quintessential great employee."

I had no idea what he was talking about, but I nodded.

Max then took us back to his list of quotes. "And the last set is about wanting a *chance*. We covered this pretty thoroughly in the gifted bosses section, but here are a few of the sentiments directly from bosses."

> They want to be tested, to almost defy you to give them something they can't handle.

> The great employees are confident employees—they seek out measurement, and want to be paid accordingly.

> The very best are always entrepreneurial. You have to come up with new projects just to keep them interested.

This last section disappointed me because it seemed so distant from my situation as to be irrelevant. I told my companion, "I know you talked about this earlier, but I'm still unclear on how I can get—or give—chunks of responsibility within an organization."

"The best employees," Max began, "are show-offs. They know they're good and want a chance to prove it. They want to get into the game. It's not easy figuring out how to give employees that chance. You somehow have to figure out how to harness entrepreneurial energy without them leaving the company. It's not uncommon to hear a manager say, 'Hire good people and get out of their way.' But many who mouth that cliché only pretend to hand over authority. They continue to make all the decisions while pretending not to, saying to employees, 'It's up to you, *but what I'd do is...*'"

I jumped in to relate an instance where a boss had said just that to me, and I had decided to go against his advice. After all, I figured, he said it was up to me. He never forgave me. Never trusted me again. And I soon left.

Max said, "I wish you could work for Larry Tree, a gifted boss who runs EMS—Equipment Maintenance Services—a company that cares for giant industrial equipment in several western states. He literally got out of the way." Max then told me this about Larry Tree:

"While EMS has hundreds of employees, they work in various facilities scattered throughout the West, and Tree has decentralized his business to the point where the headquarters staff consists of just four people. And one of his facilities kicked him out of their building. He had his corporate office in one of the regional facilities, and when they needed more space, he moved his staff into a trailer.

"And, truly having gotten out of the way, Tree is free to devote his time to strategy, acquisitions and to what he calls 'culture development.' He says, 'We are always working on the culture. It's better to be consciously incompetent than unconsciously competent.' And then he laughed and asked me, 'Does that make sense?' Now that's my kind of boss.

"Part of that culture is Tree telling the employees 'Live your dream.' He wants to know the personal dreams of employees and then tries to find a place where they align with the company goals.

"He has harnessed the energies of the entrepreneurial employees by dividing the company into pieces, and regarding the employees who run them as 'CEOs.' One of them, who runs the Wyoming facility, started the company as an hourly employee. Tree says, 'He was a machinist, hired by someone who left the company long ago. I saw his talents, and I encouraged him to dream. I kept finding new assignments for him, to test him, because I wanted to see just how good he could be. He's now CEO of a ten-million-dollar facility and brings twenty percent to the bottom line. I don't think I could do that.' Now that's a great employee, allowed to blossom working with a gifted boss."

But I was back to my old concern, that the example he'd given had little relation to my situation, working inside a company where I had little latitude. Max laughed, saying, "You have a latitude attitude." And he gave my knee another of his viselike grips. The poor thing was starting to be a tad tender.

"So here's an example you'll have to like," Max said. "David Wing spent most of his career managing retail stores and now runs Retail Advisors, a consulting business for retailers. This is what he tells store owners . . . I'm quoting Wing:

" 'Treat people as "employees" and that's what you get. And they leave as soon as they can get fifty cents an hour more somewhere else. But treat them as coworkers and everything changes. Make them part of the business, not just employees. You do that by giving them a part of the operation to run. For instance, you put one employee in charge of displays, or men's shirts, or the check-in process. And you get them to learn by teaching. I'd have weekly meetings with discussion topics. I'd say to an employee, "I want to have a meeting on displays, and I want you to run it." Once I had an employee who had a gift for turning returns into new sales. If someone wanted to return an item, they'd always walk out with even more than they brought back. So I told her I wanted her to teach everyone else to do it. She had to figure out just what she was doing in order to teach it. She made us all better.' "

Max waited for my reaction, and I admitted that it *did* apply to my situation. So Max elaborated: "In fact, Wing argues that giving employees 'ownership,' and the chance to prove themselves, is so potent a motivator that withdrawing it becomes the only 'punishment' necessary. He says, 'Say "Jane" screws up to the point that you have to do something. Move her out of her area. She'll come in to work and she'll keep looking over at "John" in her area, thinking, My God, he's touching my merchandise. He's messing up my displays. She'll never make that mistake again.' "

Then Max concluded by saying, "Most employees want more responsibility and more authority—that is, they want a promotion and a raise. But the great employees want literal or figurative ownership. They know they're good, and want the chance to prove it."

During the conversation, we had eaten a first-rate dinner, and we were having coffee when Max recalled for me one of his familiar themes. He said, "Most workplaces are like grade school. A few are like college." He added, "One is about rules and about prodding; the other is about freedom and discovery, about pulling... or at least it should be. Don't get me started on the fact that most universities are not much more than job training centers. Which reminds me of an example that involved a literal college."

Max's example was of Norm Brinker, who created and built the Steak & Ale chain, next presided over the turnaround at Burger King, then built Brinker International (Chili's restaurants, plus Cozymel's, On the Border, and Macaroni Grill). This is how Max told his story:

"Brinker only looked for a job once—when he was graduating from San Diego State. He was every recruiter's dream—a personable young man who on one hand had been on the Olympic equestrian team, but on the other hand worked his way through school selling Cutco knives. So Brinker had plenty of job prospects, including offers from P&G and Bethlehem Steel. Day after day he came to his wife and said, 'Well, honey, they offered me a job but it just didn't sound like fun—so I said, "Probably not." '

"Instead of going with a major corporation, Brinker chose a local chain of coffee shops. I asked him why. He smiled as he recalled the man who would become his mentor. He said, 'All the other people from the big companies were formal, very well dressed. I went to meet with Bob Peterson, and he was wearing a brown plaid shirt and brown slacks, no tie. And he asked me, "Why should I invite you to share my dream?" Then we went into the kitchens where the employees were experimenting with new recipes, and you could feel the energy in the room. They were laughing, having fun.'

"And Brinker found himself trying to talk Peterson into hiring him—at a salary well below what he'd been offered by the major companies.

"I asked how his wife had reacted to the decision to go with laughter instead of income. 'She understood that I never worried about money. My family was poor, poor . . . but happy. And so I've always made career decisions by asking myself, Is this going to make me happier?' "

Max bounced in his seat, expanding on "happier" as the critical job search criterion. Then he continued:

"And it was a profitable decision for Brinker, as it turned out. The dreamer in plaid was also starting a hamburger chain, Jack in the Box, and he eventually let Brinker buy a piece of the new company.

"With the profits from that piece of Jack in the Box, Brinker decided to try going into business for himself. So he opened a standard coffee shop and thereby made the typical mistake of creating a typical business. And, not surprisingly, he soon grew bored. So he tried real estate, and then decided to open a new restaurant. This time he was adamant that it would be fun—for him, the employees and the customers.

"Brinker decided that if he wanted to create a new atmosphere, he'd try a new kind of employee. Until then, restaurants were mostly staffed by middle-aged men and women with low expectations and tired feet. Brinker decided he wanted younger employees, with enough style to pull off wearing Old English costumes, and enough vigor to create a new atmosphere. So he called the nearest college, Southern Methodist University, and told the placement office that he planned to hire fifteen students. The woman at the placement office was cooperative until he mentioned the name, Steak & Ale. When she learned there was liquor involved, she backed out. That's when Brinker got in his car and drove to a fraternity house. He showed pictures of the restaurant and shared his dreams, and got his staff.

"By seeking to create an environment that appealed to him, Norm Brinker invented a new segment of the restaurant business that came to be known as 'casual dining.' And he created a lively work environment where the great employees of the future—kids still in college—could be current great employees. What he had done, without intending to, was to tap into the needs of the best employees. They know they can always get a job and make money. So what do they look for when choosing a workplace? Exceptional employees are drawn to exceptional environments."

Max let me contemplate that story while he drank his coffee. Then he added one more observation about Brinker's restaurant:

"Notice that even with part-time restaurant employees, the gifted boss went out in search of great employees instead of sitting back and hoping they'd turn up. This is a case of a great boss figuring out where to go to find employees with the talents he wanted and then courting them, romancing a lively work environment."

Max stretched and said he was ready to head back to the house. "Speaking of romance," he added, "tomorrow we will explore all the amazing ways that gifted bosses find and court highly talented employees."

I saw a chance to provoke him and I took it. "Hold on. What's this 'find and court'? I thought if you created a magnetic workplace then great employees come to you."

"Ah, you've been listening after all. I'm flattered. And on the morrow you will come to understand that, yes, if you create a magnetic workplace, *some* great employees will come to you. Some just appear, usually when some idiot boss has not known how to handle real talent. But there are plenty of great employees who never even think of changing jobs. Literally. It just doesn't occur to them. Some of the best of the best are like that. You have to seek them out. And the only chance you have with them is a workplace suited to them, aka the Best Place for the Best People to Work."

The Courtship Rituals

☆ ☆ ☆ ☆ ☆

The next morning I came downstairs and found Max cooking breakfast. He was talking on a portable phone, laughing and cursing and dicing fruit at the same time. He had waffles going, and eggs. He saw me and effortlessly brought me into the work and then into his conversation, telling the person on the other end about our evening, quoting me and making me sound profound.

We sat in a breakfast room worthy of a magazine feature—colors everywhere, indoors and out, windows on two sides, beveled glass insets sending light shafts coming in to cross at angles like swords of musketeers. Later, when I said as much, Max laughed and showed me where the homeowner had a copy of a homes magazine on display, and there was our room. And that morning, as I sat down with Max, I felt as if we were worthy of photo documentation, and silently wished they'd come back to take pictures of us.

But it wasn't long before Max was back to workplaces. He said that in order to understand how gifted bosses and great employees come together, we would need to consider three of the

"Six Realities" simultaneously. He gave me another of his work-sheets, with these principles:

2. Gifted bosses don't just hire employees, they acquire allies.

3. Great employees don't have jobs, they have talents. They enter the job market once (if at all), and thereafter their talents are spotted, courted and won over.

4. Great bosses and employees often reverse the typical job search: instead of the employee doing the "hunting," it's the boss. The process more resembles a "talent search" than a "job market."

THE ALLIANCE

"I suppose I should begin," Max began, "by explaining why I use the term 'allies.' Given the fact that gifted bosses and great employees want the same thing from the workplace, it might seem that they should be called a workplace 'team.'

"You can, of course, call any group of people who report to one person a 'team'—for instance, the president's cabinet is given that label, although the members of that 'team' rarely work together; instead, they often come together to compete for resources. Likewise, the team image does not fit many of the great bosses or employees that I met. There aren't many 'group decisions,' because the gifted boss is more like an enlightened monarch than a team leader. And while gracious, helpful and cooperative, the great employees are individualists with unique talents. They are not interchangeable. And they grow impatient with committee members—and let's face it, the majority of workplace teams are just committees.

"Instead of 'teams,' the 'alliances' I observed were something other than mere employment. And it wasn't 'mentoring' because it wasn't that one-sided. It's more like a new and improved form of kinship."

He stopped to frown at me, then shook his head, acting hurt and disappointed. "Every time I get the least bit philosophical, you just tune out."

"No. Absolutely not. New form of kinship. I'm right with you."

"Well, let me give you an example, one of my favorites. And it comes from a large corporation, larger than yours, so you can't fall into your 'latitude attitude.' It's one example of a man with the fortune and skill to have worked for a great boss and with a great employee. It's a long story, so enjoy your waffle.

"In the early eighties, when he was a manager in the communications group for the videotape division of 3M, Don Linehan met his first—and only—great boss, an Italian executive who was an assistant to a high-level executive. The Italian, Edoardo Pieruzzi, had been brought in to work at 3M's St. Paul headquarters as part of an informal 'grooming' process. And that's where Pieruzzi discovered Linehan, an energetic employee who wanted to bring new life to the division, and who had ideas about how to do it. And so Pieruzzi made Linehan an ally—not by asking for help, but by giving it.

"Linehan described their early relationship: 'He was very political. He charmed the CEO and all the other top executives. His wife stayed in Italy, so he was free to work twenty-four hours, and to socialize with the executives. He was always available if an executive wanted to talk. And he would plan vacations to Europe for them—arrange every detail. So he got to know everything going on with the executives. And he would apply his political craftiness to my projects. He took my ideas and moved them to the bank.'

"In other words, the role of the gifted boss in this alliance was to be an *idea salesman*. He didn't manage the idea process, he was the agent for the department. Imagine the energy that is unleashed simply from knowing that good ideas are going to be sold to the head of the division. What better way to reinforce creativity than to see ideas blossom into innovations.

"Eventually, Pieruzzi became the VP of the video division and promoted Linehan to be the head of the communications department. One of Linehan's ideas that Pieruzzi sold to upper management was that 3M become a major Olympic sponsor. This would be a fateful project, for it was where Linehan would encounter his own great employee.

"But I'm getting ahead of myself. First, Pieruzzi was promoted again, this time to a job back in Europe. He soon had Linehan come over on business, and once there, took him to dinner at his private club in Brussels. It was there he told Linehan, 'I want you to be head of communications for Europe.'

"Linehan eagerly agreed, and with his wife and son soon moved to Brussels. What followed was what Linehan calls 'the richest years of our lives. My son went to an international school, and his class would travel by train all over Europe. When his class studied the art of Florence, they went to Florence. When my son gave his class report on Michelangelo's *David*, he gave it standing in front of the statue. My son cried when we came back. We all did.'

"What brought Linehan back was a promotion, and a job back at headquarters in St. Paul. And while he no longer reported to Pieruzzi, they remained allies. Linehan says of him, 'I still thought of him as my surrogate boss. I'd call and tell him a problem and he'd say, "Here's what's going on, and here's what you must do." He knew everything about upper management and was more valuable as a nonboss than a boss. He was my biggest supporter of global projects, and I was his biggest supporter anytime he wanted my help.'

"Pieruzzi was a mentor to Linehan, and coach and father figure and brother and friend. Instead of 'blood brothers' they are 'talent brothers'—committed not just to the other, but also to the other's potential and fulfillment.

"But let's back up to how Linehan found his own great employee.

"When Linehan put together 3M's Olympic sponsorship, there were sixty-five countries involved. Each country had its own program—advertising, promotional tie-ins and using the Games for relationship building with major customers or suppliers. Out of these sixty-five programs, one was special. It was the Canadian program, run by a young 3M employee named Bruce Moorhouse. What impressed Linehan was this: 'Not only that he used his resources wisely and creatively, but he was able to track changes in numbers. He was able to measure what the program actually accomplished. His became the model for the world.'

"And when Linehan returned from Europe, he wanted to put together a new worldwide image campaign. And so he created a task force of eight countries, and included Canada just so he could see more of Bruce Moorhouse's work. 'I had this major program in mind,' Linehan said, 'and I wanted him to be the cornerstone. It took almost a year to bring him in.' And as we shall see, the statement 'bring him in' is the sort of language that a gifted boss uses to describe the hiring of a great employee. The metaphors often involved 'searching' or 'hunting': the great employees were far more often hunted than hunters.

"And what made the young Canadian a great employee? In Linehan's words, 'You gave him a project—or okayed one he suggested—and *knew* that it would be on time, on budget, and top quality. And always with a twist, something original, a mark of individuality that made it his. That was his *brand*.'

"Interesting that Linehan, a man who made a career out of building brands for one of the most admired companies in the world, would speak of an employee's talents as a 'brand.' We often hear the advice that every employee thinks of his or her career as a 'business,' but I prefer Linehan's notion of a brand, because it suggests being one of many, and thus calling out for differentiation and image building.

"Besides the now-familiar theme of self-reliance, there is the other theme of kinship: Linehan says that he worried about Moorhouse, and often pleaded with him to work fewer hours—'mothering' him, in a sense.

"But there is another employee trait that is less often remarked upon, and it's important here because it suggests an awareness of the importance of the relationship.

Don Linehan, perhaps thinking of his own dinner in Brussels, took Moorhouse to dinner at the Waldorf to offer him the position at headquarters. Linehan knows the date: September seventeenth. He says, 'I know the date because he never let me forget it. He would tell me, "I honor that date. Thank you for hiring me. I can't believe I have this job." And he would also say, "I'll never leave, not as long as you're here."' Isn't that great? No wonder Linehan says of his great employee, 'He was a joy. A jewel.'"

Max nodded to indicate that he was finished. The story had quite an impact on me because it was just the sort of "only connect" relationship that was missing from my own work life. I could only imagine the powerful emotions of aligning myself with someone above and below, knowing that all three of us were looking out for one another. I said, "I hope that sort of thing is possible where I work. I'm afraid we aren't 3M."

"Don't worry. Yes, the quality of people at 3M is extraordinarily high. But with that in mind, I think that there's one more lesson in Don Linehan's story. In his decades at 3M, he had dozens of good employees and one great one. And he counted them up for me, and he had fourteen bosses, but formed an alliance with just one. One. Of course, maybe his standards were raised by being at such a magnetic place. Even so, the point is that alliances are too rare. But you will find them if you believe in them, if you long for them, and devote yourself to being worthy of them."

"You make it sound almost mystical."

"Not mystical, at least not to me. Maybe a 'high calling.' A different class . . . a 'noblesse oblige'? Those musketeers you mentioned would understand the rare combination of solemn duty and playfulness that grows out of a deep professional kinship. I once tried to write a family motto and came up with this: 'To live with honor and dignity, and not be too damn sanctimonious about it.' That's the same sort of feeling you get from these alliances."

"I want one...or two or three," I insisted.

"Well, the easiest place to start is with finding a great employee you can practice being gifted on. You told me before that the changes you intend to make will scare off some of your current employees. Let's talk about how you'll replace them."

THE SPOTTING AND COURTING

Max began by quoting the great coach Don Shula when he was asked about the role of "luck" in his victories. Shula had replied, "Sure, luck means a lot. Not having a good quarterback is bad luck."

Max explained: "Gifted bosses are not content to sit back and hope that great employees are sent over by Human Resources. They are masters of spotting and courting talent." And then he gave me some examples.

The "Mole"

"There's an architect named Randy Chamberlain—fascinating man—who runs Habitat, a company that operates throughout the country, designing retail stores, restaurants, sales offices, signs, model homes."

Max was in ecstasy, describing the creativity of Habitat's projects. Then he said, "A few years back, one of the company's major clients was a homebuilder whose marketing director was a former accountant, Paul Brunoforte. Working on Brunoforte's projects, Randy Chamberlain had a feeling about him. As he told me, 'You have to develop the ability to look into a second level, to see people at another level of reality.' And he came to believe that he'd spotted the ideal person to bring financial structure to Habitat."

Grabbing my forearm, he added, "But he also knew that Brunoforte had no interest in leaving his employer, which was twenty times larger than Habitat. So Randy Chamberlain undertook a talent courtship. For instance, when Habitat fell behind schedule on one of Brunoforte's projects, Chamberlain and his staff worked through the weekend, installing signs in time for the opening of a new model home complex. Not only did they work through the weekend, but through a storm. Chamberlain took photos of his exhausted team and gave them to Brunoforte. 'I wanted him to see the pride we had in the company,' Chamberlain said. 'I wasn't trying to show him what we went through, but who we were. I was courting him.' He's the only executive I've met who actually used the word *courting*—and it fits perfectly."

Max continued: "Anyway, Chamberlain held off on speaking to Brunoforte about working together. For two years, he held off. He told me, 'I was waiting for the right timing. I knew other people who knew Paul. I even had a spy in the company. He was to advise me when the time was right to approach him. And one day I got a call: "You ought to talk to Paul today." And I did.'

Max ended his story theatrically, poking the air, "Paul Brunoforte is now president of Habitat."

As I listened to Max, I could see how the word *courtship* applied. I'd met a few people in my life who'd told me romantic stories along the lines of, "I saw her across the park one day and knew she was the one for me. Three years later we married." Not having experienced such a revelation, I suspected it was some sort of hormonal coincidence, a chemical version of a lunar eclipse. But here was a business leader following the courtship model. Taken together with the 3M guys, I was beginning to see that Max was right when he accused me of going into the game with a team of "walk-ons." And at that instant it hit me, a cold fear: What if some of the other division heads in the company were finding employees the way Max was describing? What if comparable divisions at competitors were out "courting" the best talent? If so, what was I getting? Leftovers? The best employees never got to the labor pool where I went for employees. No wonder that despite all my efforts to bring innovation to our division, we still didn't "dazzle" the way I hoped we would.

Max had my full attention.

The "Warehouse"

"This is another of my favorite examples," Max said. "Bobette Gorden now runs a speakers bureau called NewInformation Presentations. Before starting her company, she was a sales rep for radio stations, and she recalled for me how it was she came to work for a gifted boss.

"'He was the manager for a radio station, one of the biggest in town. And I went to talk to him about a job, although he didn't have an opening. He called the head of another station—his best friend—and said he was sending me over. And I started working there. Later, I found out that he knew his best friend was looking for work and would be leaving, sooner or later. And so he put me there, let me get some experience and watched to see if he was right about me. He followed my progress, stayed in touch. Then, a year later, hired me—right after his friend resigned. He let someone else train me, and at the same time, he warehoused me, till he could bring me over.'

"Isn't that great?" Max said. "First we have one boss who spends two years bringing someone in, using a 'mole' to choose the right time. And now we have another boss who 'warehouses' an employee for a year. This is not your ordinary job market, is it?"

And with that Max slapped the table, saying, "Oh, I just remembered another good one. This has the record for the longest courtship I've encountered. Have you heard of a company called Solectron?"

"Sounds familiar. Didn't they win a Baldridge Award?"

"Good. Yes. Two of them, in fact. It's a five-billion-dollar-a-year business, but few people have heard of Solectron because they don't have their own brands; they manufacture products for other companies. But here's the story: A man named Winston Chen worked at IBM for many years, and got to be close to his boss, Ko Nishimura. Well, Chen takes the job running Solectron, at the time, a small company. But after he leaves IBM, he still maintains his friendship with his old boss. The two of them frequently have lunch or dinner, and Chen keeps pulling his old boss in—maybe I should say 'reeling him in.' Here is how Ko Nishimura described to me his relationship with Chen during the ten years they did not work together:

" 'He started out by asking me for my advice—"Gee, what do you think?" or "Gee, what should I do about this—any suggestions?" Like he needed my advice. And somewhere during the ten years, his question changed to "Gee, why don't you help me run the company?"

" 'But IBM had been good to me. They paid for me to get a doctorate at Stanford, something I never could have done otherwise. And I continued to learn. I had commitments. But by the mid-eighties, I felt I couldn't contribute any more . . . structure issues. I began to feel that I could help most by leaving. And so when Winston brought up again about me helping him run the company, I showed an interest. He said, "Come over and we'll figure out who'll do what." And I did. He was the boss and I was chief operating officer, and that was fine with me.' "

Max tapped my arm, adding, "Do you see how Chen kept involved with his old boss? How Chen educated Nishimura about Solectron, not by pushing information on him, but by asking for advice? That's how the best salespeople sell, by the way—with questions. And notice how Chen kept the job offer open for ten years, till Ko was ready to take it? And how he custom fit the job to this old friend? Eventually Chen retired, and Nishimura replaced him as CEO and then chairman. In the years since Nishimura came, the company has grown from less than a hundred million dollars in revenues, to over five billion. And yet Nishimura remains modest, giving credit to his old employee/boss, saying, 'I just continued what he started.' "

I appreciated the story but wasn't eager to get involved in decade-long courtships. "Does it always take so long?" I asked, trying not to sound pleading.

Max smiled. "My impatient young friend. Well, yes and no. The idea is that you are always looking for talent. Your job as a gifted boss is to be a talent scout. And once you spot talent, you start to build a relationship. So it might take years to spot the right person and years to build a relationship. Once you have the process going, it's going—there's a 'pipeline' of job candidates you're watching. And then it just happens naturally. For instance Dave Ridley, the VP of marketing for Southwest Airlines, told me that he'd been very impressed by one of the interns that worked in his department one summer. But, no openings that summer. Ridley kept in touch with the kid. Two years later, he had a perfect fit and finally brought him in. It can happen overnight, or it can take a decade."

I told Max that I could picture myself creating a file on every talented person in my industry. That I was not just a scout, but the Director of Player Personnel.

Max replied, "You just reminded me of a great conversation I had with Lou Holtz, the football coach. Let me digress a second to tell you about the gifted boss in his own career: Woody Hayes. Holtz told me a number of stories about being an assistant to Hayes, but the most striking was that the whole time he knew him, Hayes turned down every raise he was offered, saying, 'Give it to the assistants, they have families to raise.' Can you imagine?"

"No," I said simply.

Max smiled. "We have miles to go. Anyway, back to hiring. Holtz told me this:

" 'You can't just wait till there's an opening and say, "Who can we hire?" That's how you end up with a group of second-stringers. Say you hire ten guys. If you're lucky, five are good. So all the responsibility gravitates to the five. They resent it. And they are also the ones who are attractive to other schools. So you end up replacing them with five more. And, say, two of those are good. Over time, you end up with all second-stringers.' "

"So," I asked, "what did Holtz recommend? Do you hire twenty?"

"No," Max countered quickly, then pulled a face, reconsidering. "Well, in a way, I guess it was a bigger number than that. What Holtz did was keep a hiring list. On it were prospects who would fit every job he had. For someone to make the list was like being halfway to hired—although nobody knew about the existence of that list. Remember, these jobs weren't even open; but he kept the list, just in case. Whenever he'd hear about a good assistant, he'd keep an eye on the guy, try to get to know him well enough to know if he wanted to work with him, and to know how to win him over. So when an opening appeared, Holtz knew the man he wanted and how to court him. He knew who wanted to be a head coach and who wanted to go to the NFL and so on. He didn't say, 'Come and help me,' but 'Here's how I can help you get what you want.' And he established a track record of doing just that. Holtz has former assistants all over the NCAA and NFL."

My first reaction was to think that it would be a mistake to let a great assistant go, but then it occurred to me that it would be a lot easier to help employees move on if you had a list of replacements.

"By the way," I asked Max, "did Holtz ever tell you what he looked for in an assistant?"

"He told me he looked for a 'natural teacher' and then said with real intensity, "The great coaches are fun to be around... they *laugh!*' " Which, naturally, set Max to laughing.

I was eager to get my scouting under way, although I voiced one concern: "It sounds like it could take years to run across these prospects for great employees. Any way to speed things up?"

"Not years. I suspect that if you look at all the people you come in contact with, you'll have some prospects immediately. You won't be surprised to hear that I have a story on that subject."

The Reversal

Max then told me of Erik Saltvold:

"He's just thirty-three, but he's been in business for twenty years. As a high school student, he started a bike sales and repair business for a work-study project. Growing up, Saltwold lived with his family in an old farmhouse, and it had an unused barn, which he converted into a showroom. He bought used bikes, fixed then resold them. Soon—he was just fourteen, at this point—he decided to stock new bikes. So he went to a wholesaler to make his first buy. The fellow asked his name. 'Erik,' he replied.

" 'Not *your* name, the company name.'

" 'I don't have one.'

" 'Well, I need to put down something. How about Erik's Bike Shop?'

"And by age fifteen Eric had a real bike shop in the barn, and was having his mom drive him into Minneapolis to the wholesaler where he would order thousands of dollars of merchandise.

"The company name hasn't changed, but Erik's Bike Shop now has six locations in the Twin Cities and a hundred and fifty employees. And those employees have come from Erik's recruiting of salespeople.

"It makes sense. The best salespeople are heavily involved with bikes. Saltvold says, 'It's a "techie" sport and there are people who love to tinker with bikes. And it's not a get-rich industry, so you have to love bikes to work in it. There is a fairly small pool of individuals with the interests and background. Where do you find potential employees with those characteristics? They come in the store all day long.' Saltvold told me, 'I've hired so many customers that all the managers know to look at customers as potential employees. When they get to know one that would fit into our company, they ask, "How would you like to work with us?" In other words, the customers become salespeople, and the salespeople become managers.' "

This story did not seem as relevant to my situation, because I don't have customers in the same sense as a retail operation. But by this point, I could tumble to Max's broader point: in this case, look at everyone you come in contact with. I found myself thinking of one young woman who worked for one of our consultants . . . a great employee.

"Did I lose you?" Max asked.

"I just started thinking of a possible candidate. She definitely qualifies as a Wild Brain. A true innovator. She'd be fabulous in my department, but she's got a good job now. I doubt I could even match her salary, much less beat it."

Max made a show of tearing a piece of paper off his pad and then wadding it up and pitching it at my head. "There you go, back into the glass rut, thinking in the average way about the average hiring process. First, they all have good jobs, the great employees. Almost all, anyway. But get to know this prospect. Find out what she really wants to work on. She may be dreaming of a project that would revolutionize how you work. Remember: freedom, a change and a chance. The old school is to hire someone you need by offering twenty percent more money. Well, try offering a hundred percent more freedom or a hundred percent more excitement. Remember Norm Brinker being hired by the 'dreamer in brown plaid.' You need to get yourself free to dream and then find a dream to share."

He was right. As soon as I'd pictured myself with this prize catch of an employee, my excitement had caused me to fall back on familiar thinking. Now I was thinking of what I could accomplish with an alliance.

The Antibureaucrat Goes Hiring

With his eyes twitching in anticipation, Max declared, "Now I'm going to tell you a story that will shake up your thinking. You cannot be in a glass rut and do what Ron Walters did. He was running a sales office for a national printing company. He'd met a person at another firm whom he really wanted to hire and had worked at getting to know. One day she told him she was ready to change jobs . . . immediately. He did not have an opening, or any money in the budget. But he hired her anyway. For the first month he paid her out of his own pocket. Now there's someone working in a bureaucracy who refused to think like a bureaucrat."

I confess I found myself refusing to consider doing something comparable.

Max saw my consternation, and added, "Ron Walters was building a team and he knew that a great employee would return wealths to him. Not just wealth, but wealths. And, by the way, I should tell you a little more about this guy. He eventually left the big firm and started his own company, Freedom Printing, and built it to a multi-million-dollar operation in just a few years. He created a magnetic workplace, and one way he insured that it was the best place to work was that he would encourage his employees to look for other jobs and to come back and tell him what they found out there. Over the years, many took him up on that suggestion. He learned a lot—it was 'competitive intelligence'—but the goal was to be certain that they weren't offering a better workplace. And he never once lost an employee in the process."

Max stopped himself. "But I'm digressing. I wanted to tell you about his other hiring strategy. Besides just spotting people he came in contact with, he would ask his customers who they would like to work with. You could do the same. I know, I know. You don't have the same kind of customers."

He stopped again, this time to narrow his eyes and say, "Don't make me wad up another piece of paper."

I held up my hands. "No need. I'm not thinking like a bureaucrat. What I'm going to do is go to the people in our company in other departments and ask them about people they've worked with at previous employers. I'm thinking of a brand manager who recently came over from Intel. There might be a great employee at Intel in a department comparable to mine, whom I could contact. Maybe arrange to meet at one of the conventions or somewhere. Start tracking that person. Maybe we don't pay more than Intel, but in my department, at least, we're going to have more freedom, energy and excitement."

Max stood and gave me a bow.

"'Okay. You've got it," Max said, delighted. "You are now an official talent scout. I loved your idea of having a file on every great prospect in the country, or maybe the world. So, let me ask you now a question I asked you on the phone when we first started all this. What's your philosophy of hiring?"

I had an answer: "My department will be—no, make that 'is becoming'—the best place for the best people to work. And it's my job to let the best people know. Hiring isn't something you do when an employee quits. And it happens mostly outside the job market. A lot of great employees never look for jobs. So I need to spot them and court them. And since I'll be freed from most managing chores, I can devote myself to scouting, to networking."

"Very good. I have just one quibble. I wish you'd ended that statement two words sooner. To me, 'scouting' and 'networking' are different. You could go to a thousand luncheons and never come away with a great employee, or a great boss, either. You could have five thousand names on a Rolodex, and all it would accomplish is to keep you too busy to seek out great employees. I'm not interested in cultivating contacts, in being able to pick up the phone and get tickets to some Broadway show. That's fine if you want to do it. But the scouting process isn't just getting to know a lot of people, it's getting to know the work of highly talented people."

Seeing a Lot of Games

"And to continue the analogy a bit further," Max said, "the best talent scout is going to see a lot of games, see a lot of prospects. One way to do that is to have worked with a lot of people. So this is one instance where older is better ... *if* the person has been spotting talent all along, and keeping in touch. We'll talk later about how talented people keep recycling one another.

"But there are ways for someone in your position to start spotting talent. And you might want to emphasize young talent, because great employees rise so quickly that it's hard to get them later on. So you can hire interns. Or teach a college class. I've known several professionals who do this not just to be stimulated by young minds but also to spot the best young talent. That was another of the tricks of John Genzale, our poetry man. He's recruited so many rising journalists that the publisher of the main paper in town went to the dean and complained that they were 'tired of getting Genzale's leftovers.'

"And speaking of colleges—they went one step further at Marketplace Ministries in Dallas. This is a fascinating company— they place corporate chaplains in companies around the country. They have about five hundred of them."

I expressed my doubts about religion being mixed in with corporate life. Max countered, saying, "I know what you mean. But it's not like that. The founder, Gil Stricklin, was an air force chaplain, and it's all nondenominational. The idea is to have someone around the office or factory that you can *really* talk to. The idea is so powerful that one of the key employees is a man who left a New York ad agency and took a cut in pay of over one hundred grand. Talk about a magnetic workplace!

"Anyway, don't let me digress. My point is that Gil—the founder—did more than teach a class. He helped a big seminary in Dallas create a master of corporate chaplaincy—the first in the world, as far as I know. His goal was to boost the concept, but there was a marvelous unintended consequence: He has cre- ated a flow of talent. He helped create a graduate program that finds and trains potential employees. And all the students do an internship with Gil's firm. So he gets to see them all in action. In effect, he grows his own talent, and the crop pays to be grown."

My lack of immediate response was enough to get Max to jump in and say, "Okay, okay, you're going to tell me that it's not in your power to create a new graduate program. I'm not sure that's true, but let's go with the assumption. How's this: College professors love their students to work on real-world pro- jects. You get some work done for free, or almost free, and you get to work with potential recruits. You see their minds at work."

"That I could do with a phone call. A professor approached me last year, and I put him off."

"Remind me to give you a quarter for the call," he said, playing at sarcasm. But then he was going on: "Or, you might try temps. There are executive temps now, so you can 'try out' employees. But you can also use lower-level temps as a source of trainees for higher-level positions. I've known executives—for instance, Bryan Stauning of Information Management Systems in Minneapolis—who prefer to use a lot of temps in the clerical roles, not because they don't have enough work for full-timers, but because they want a chance to spot great employees, ones they'll hire and train for other positions.

"Oh, one more," Max said, reinvigorating himself with a recollection. "I have got to tell you about Susan and Barry Brooks, who own a mail-order gift business called Cookies from Home. Barry was interviewing for a part-time supervisor, and in comes an older man that Susan describes as looking as if he were wearing one of those Groucho masks. Turns out that he's a retired executive, looking for something to get him out of the house. His name is Vince Ciccarelli, and he was a turnaround specialist in New York. Instead of giving him the job he was applying for—production supervisor—they hire him to review their operations. And soon Barry and Susan fall in love with the guy's business wisdom. So Barry offers him a permanent job, but Ciccarelli turns it down, saying that he has decided to go back into retirement. And then he goes into Susan's office to tell her of his decision and to say good-bye. Well, Susan Brooks is not the sort of person you say no to. As he's talking, she walks over and closes her office door, then, standing in front of it, arms out, she announces, 'You can't leave. I don't care if you work an hour a day or ten, but you're not leaving till you agree to work for us. We need you.'

Ciccarelli's reaction was to throw back his head and laugh. Susan described that moment, that laugh, by saying, 'I knew then that I could give him what he needed—to be needed.' "

Max continued: "And here's where the story gets even more interesting. She told him that he could set his own conditions of employment—whatever he wanted. And he came back and said that he wanted to leave every day at three o'clock, and on Fridays at noon. And then he told the owners of the company that he wanted them to report to him. He said, 'You can fire me any time you want, but you work for me.' And Susan and Barry agreed, which tells you something about them as gifted bosses. That decision paid off—their revenues had been stagnant before Ciccarelli joined them; it's doubled in the three years since."

As Max spoke I was struck by how far my own attempts at hiring had been from those of Susan Brooks or Lou Holtz or the others. My efforts were, by comparison, cold—not just impersonal but self-centered. I'd never taken the time to figure out what employees wanted from life, just how much I could offer. And by using the traditional methods, I would never ever have seen a retired gem of an employee, much less tried to put together a work relationship suited to such a person.

The Discounters

Max stopped and stared at me. "What?" I said, waiting to be accused of something less than full attention. But he was lost in his own recollections. "Oh, just that there was one other source I wanted to suggest." He grimaced and then said, "Oh, yes. I like this one. And if you're ready to take a few chances, you might like it too. It's the 'damaged goods' approach. Sometimes you can pick up a great employee who would normally be unavailable, someone who should be at a much higher level. I hired one guy who had been fired from another company after his wife left him and he'd gone into a depression. A drinking problem. I told him, 'If you beat it, I'll hire you.' That was the ray of hope he needed. And he recovered and has worked for me ever since. Brilliant and completely loyal to our alliance.

"And I met a man who worked within a big corporation who had a collection of Wild Brains he had assembled. He confided in me that it was easy. What he did was hire troublemakers, people other managers were about to give up on because they were difficult to manage. He established his department as a place for 'difficult people.' They weren't difficult for him, because he set them loose instead of trying to manage them, and they turned out amazing work. Another case of a person in the middle of a big bureaucracy who managed to turn the disadvantages of size to his favor."

The Old Methods Made New

We discussed how I could apply these strategies to my hiring. When I thought we were finished with the subject, Max announced that he wanted to cover one last point.

"It was important to break through your glass rut and get you thinking like a talent scout. Mostly you'll search out talent; occasionally it will drop on you. Either way, you keep the pipeline flowing. But there are situations where you don't have anyone in the pipeline and you need to do some instant scouting/hiring."

Max then told me of John Kilcullen, the CEO of IDG Books, the folks who've had the incredible success of the *For Dummies* series of books.

"After the company's early success, John wanted to hire a financial genius. So instead of bringing in a search firm, he calls the head of the biggest industry convention and asks, 'Who's the best financial mind in publishing?' And his answer was 'Steve Berkowitz.' Then Kilcullen gets the convention guy to tell Berkowitz, 'You should meet each other.' Then, when the convention comes along, Kilcullen arranges to take an afternoon off to play golf with Berkowitz. Kilcullen is no golfer—in fact, he showed up in blue jeans, which aren't allowed in the course's dress code, so he ended up playing in linen dress pants, which he ruined. But Kilcullen was willing to make a fool of himself, trying to play, just to have four or five hours to get to know the guy, to interview him without his knowing it. They hit it off, and then it was time for Kilcullen to begin the courtship.

"Turns out the biggest obstacle was getting Berkowitz, and his wife—especially his wife—to leave Long Island. So Kilcullen flies cross-country to New York, rents a car and drives to their home, so he can sit down with them both and persuade them to come to California to take a look. And they did, and were hooked."

Max stopped himself to smile at me, reading in my face that I'd profited from that example. I asked him for more examples, and he told me of Leroy Cook, who heads a national referral network for private investigators. He needed to hire someone quickly and decided to run a newspaper ad. But, being a gifted boss, he didn't run an ordinary ad. He had tried those in the past and was disappointed with the quality of people who applied. So he decided to run an ad that began WANTED: SUPERMAN OR WONDER WOMAN and described a great employee. He didn't get many responses but did tap into a whole new level of interesting candidates. In fact, readers of the classifieds were tearing out the ad to give to people they thought were great employees.

Max jumped ahead: "Another, related case was from a guy I mentioned earlier, Ron Walters and his printing company. He's the one who paid a new employee out of his own pocket. Well, he needed a 'temp.' But when he calls the agency, he says, 'Don't send the usual person. Send someone special.' And they did. It's remarkable what you can get just by asking. It turns out that the temp was a woman who had just moved to town. She's a great employee and knows it. And so she was working as a temp in order to 'try out' companies. She spots Ron as a great boss and goes to him and says, 'What would it take to get hired here?' That's a great example of a great employee taking the initiative, and it's also an example of how, every once in a while, a great employee falls from the heavens."

I responded by saying, "I suppose that the trick is to recognize them when they fall."

Max nodded and said, "Sometimes you get just a glimpse. Which takes us to Gary Lannigan. When he was marketing director for a shipbuilding company, he was walking past the front desk and overheard a woman talking to the receptionist. The woman was explaining that she had just read a newspaper article about the company and how fast it was growing, so she thought they might have a job for her. The receptionist turns her down like a bedspread."

I laughed at that image, and Max gave credit for the line to P. G. Wodehouse. "Anyway, the receptionist sends this woman away. But Lannigan recognizes the initiative. He sees someone who didn't rely on typical techniques, and he's wise enough to know that the best employees are not typical. So he stops her as she's leaving and learns that she's been out of the job market for twenty years, raising a family, and now she's ready to work again. The upshot is that Lannigan hires her and gives her the receptionist's job."

Max stopped and said, "So there it is. You learn to be a scout, you plan your employee 'mergers and acquisitions' and then you keep your mind open, hoping to get the occasional gift from the old methods."

I nodded, eager to get started. I was looking forward to Monday, when I would be back in the office and I could start designing my magnetic workplace and start my prospect files.

"There are two more subjects," Max said, "and then we'll stop talking about business and do some sight-seeing. And the next topic is"—at this he leaned in and spoke in a hammy whisper—"the secret skill. Shhhh."

The Secret Skill

★ ★ ★ ★ ★

We stopped long enough to clean up the kitchen and to move back onto the patio. Sparrows flitted in the branches of Palo Verde trees, and the sun was skittering through the lacy branches, warming us as we sat. Max passed over another sheet of paper with one of his principles.

> 5. While many gifted bosses have created such special work environments that they have virtually no turnover, many others embrace substantial turnover and become masters of "the secret skill" of firing.

Sounding unusually somber, he said, "Nowhere in my research did I find such a dichotomy among gifted bosses as in their attitudes toward employee turnover and firings. More than half of the gifted bosses have substantial turnover and don't mind. Indeed, they welcome it, causing much of it themselves, by "letting go" a substantial proportion of their staffs. However, many others—at least one-third of the bosses—have virtually no turnover."

I offered this observation: "It seems to me that a gifted boss would fit the latter case. After all, a wise boss selects employees wisely and then creates a marvelous work environment that people don't want to leave."

"Yes. True. But there is a competing logic. A great boss sets high standards and isn't afraid to admit that employees often fall short. Also, it can be exhausting working at such a high level, and employees often opt for a softer environment. Result: substantial turnover."

"Or," I added, "maybe they didn't do such a good job of talent scouting."

Max grinned and nodded. "You're right. If you hire people on hunches, rather than seeing their work over time, you'll make mistakes.

"Either way," he continued, "there are two ways to think about turnover. Some companies merely focus on the cost of hiring and training employees and assume that the less turnover the better. But the right kind of turnover can actually be quite healthy. If a company sets high standards and rewards excellence, and the result is that twenty percent of the employees leave each year, that company will grow mighty—they will be like the title of the book Joe Namath wrote many years ago, *I Can't Wait Until Tomorrow...'Cause I Get Better Looking Every Day*."

Max digressed a while about Namath but then resumed, saying, "On the other hand, if the company is inept or has a dreadful work environment, it's the best employees who can most easily move on, and so even a small turnover becomes disastrous because it is from the top, a 'brain drain.' The upshot is that the company with twenty percent turnover can be much healthier than the one with ten percent turnover."

I asked Max if that really happened.

"There is research on healthy turnover under the rubric 'functional turnover,'" he replied. "But the best way to understand the concept is to look at some of the most admired companies in the country. For example, while Southwest Airlines is famous for its hiring practices, no one says much about its firing practices—but you should know that they consider the first six months a trial period in which any employee can be fired at will, and that includes union employees. And Nordstrom loses nearly a quarter of its salespeople each year. The leaders of the company accept such turnover—maybe even welcome it—regarding it as a natural selection process."

Here I stopped Max to question him about the wisdom of that approach.

He responded, "One of the sayings at Nordstrom is 'Your performance is your review.' Given that much of the employee's income is from commissions, and that expectations for hard work are very high, the employees tend to select themselves out. In fact, one of the advantages of having a great employee or two around is that they can make firing irrelevant. Remember the executive with the shipbuilder, Gary Lannigan? One day he went into the company facilities on a Sunday, the day before they were planning to take some boats to a major trade show. And while walking through, Lannigan came across a lone employee—a young man, a recent immigrant, who was finishing work on a boat. As they talked, Lannigan realized that this kid had exceptional personal standards, that he was doing work beyond the company's usual level of preparation. And so the next day Lannigan tells the president, 'Take care of this kid.' "

I found myself wondering how often it happens that a young kid who doesn't speak English very well has two key executives watching over him. Max concluded the story by saying, "So the kid gets promoted and promoted and finally goes off to join a major shipbuilder. But the story doesn't end there. The kid—now middle-aged—started his own company. And the big company he left missed him so much, they went to him and bought his company just to get him back. Now that's a great employee. When I asked Lannigan just what traits this guy had, his answers were all about high standards. And then he said something I hadn't heard from anyone else but I suspect is true elsewhere. He said, 'I never had to fire anybody after he came to work for us. He would scare off all the people who didn't aspire to being the best.'"

He gave me time to contemplate that.

"Still," he continued, "despite the high standards and the presence of other great employees as role models or scarecrows, a large number of gifted bosses do a lot of firing. What surprised me was, when I was able to get some of them to open up about their firing practices, that they are masters of shedding unwanted employees, often doing it so gracefully that the ex-employee remains an ally of the firm, and sometimes even returns. Here's another example from John Genzale:

"John told me of the time when he was leaving the *Miami News* and the staff had a going-away party for him. *Seven of the people he had fired* showed up. When I asked if they had come to 'dance on his grave,' he laughed. 'No, they wanted to wish me well. They all knew that I had always wished them well and that I tried to help them. I never sacrificed a person's dignity, and never fired a person who deep down didn't know it wasn't working out.'

"I asked for an example. He told me of a woman who had consistently violated one of the company policies. He talked, then pleaded, then threatened. Finally, he told her, 'The next time, I'm going to have to fire you.' And when the next time came, he told her sadly, 'I love you, but it's over.' The event was so expected, so de-emotionalized, that she reacted by asking to use Genzale's phone. She proceeded to use his phone to postpone an appointment with her hairdresser. And he then helped her think through her career options, and helped her find another job.

"But Genzale also gave me an example of a person he did *not* fire. 'We had an older guy, a real gentleman, who was nearing seventy, and the company had no mandatory retirement age. He was over the hill. I knew I should replace him with a better person. But he had no family, just a dog. The paper and the dog, that was his whole life. I couldn't fire him. Would we be better off replacing him? Yes. Would we be better people? No.' "

Max added, "That story illustrates the role of firings in the culture of the company. I've known companies to keep on employees who are struggling—health, family, drinking, drugs—the company holding off, trying to help. I once told the story about the paper and the dog to a writer in Albuquerque, Tony Lesce. And he told me he'd worked for a newspaper publisher, a great boss, who had an employee with a drinking problem. 'Occasionally, this guy would pass out. We would step over him, there on the floor. But the publisher wouldn't fire him because he felt the employee would turn around. It was one reason we all loved this publisher—he cared that much about his people.' "

Max stopped to shrug, a gesture that didn't fit him. He added, "This was years ago. I'm not certain that someone would do the same today. And, once again, there is logic on the other side. Larry Tree, the CEO who moved the headquarters staff into a trailer, told me, 'One way to reward a performer is to admonish a nonperformer. The employees think, Hey, management notices.

They care. When you ignore mediocrity, the bar is lowered. Then it's okay to do less.' "

Max quietly continued: "And Ken Donahue of Teledyne admitted to me sadly that firing can be 'an important management tool.' What he means is that you use firing and hiring to set new standards, to demonstrate to other employees what you are looking for. After three years without sales growth, he replaced his head of sales, and sales went up sixty percent. He says, 'People are smart, they pick up on it. Employees look at that and think, "I understand—here's the performance and work ethic that's rewarded." And they look at the person who left and think, "And there's the performance and work ethic that is unacceptable." It's part of the process of getting people to understand what the company wants. You see people who are out, and know what they would have done. And you see people who are new, and know what they are doing. Before long you don't have to ask: You know it, feel it—this is what the company would want me to do.'

"So," Max said, leaning in, "these bosses accept the need to fire people. But that doesn't mean they jump to it. As Ken Donahue put it, 'If it's easy to fire someone, it's probably the wrong decision.' What he meant was that if it's easy, you're not caring enough. He also argued that treating people with dignity sends another type of message: 'Employees want to know that if they have to leave, they'll be able to feed their families, have the time to find a new job.' "

With this, Max returned to his old self, bouncing in his seat and saying, "Angelo Petrilli is one of the gifted bosses who does more than give departing employees time, he gives them his help. 'I tell them, "I know you've done your best, but you haven't found what you were meant to do." And then I help them focus on their strengths and weaknesses, and then try to use my network to help them find a new job.' He also admitted, 'Sometimes I feel like I'm a headhunter.' But time and caring comes back to gifted bosses—instead of making enemies, they actually make allies with those they've fired. Norm Brinker told me this, 'If you care, you attract quality people. Winners attract winners and leaders attract leaders. But sometimes people aren't performing and they've got to go. You deal with it kindly and with compassion. You help them to do better in the next job. At one point, I had so many people I had fired who became regular customers, that one of the managers told me, "You've got to fire more people; it's good for sales." ' "

Max told me several stories of fired employees who ended up being hired back. He recounted cases of gifted bosses who had employees who have left two or three times. They leave and try something new, and come back grateful and recharged. Here I interrupted long enough to add a personal example. While I'm not trying to horn in on the "gifted boss" category, on this one occasion I got it right. When I ran a division of a market research company, I had a young Colombian woman working for me. Suddenly, she lost interest in her work, became absentminded, missed deadlines, and so on. She had fallen in love. I told myself that I'd "lost her to Cupid," which was charming ... at first. Months passed and she never regained her interest. After many discussion sessions, I had to fire her. I could only console myself with the knowledge that it was best for the company and maybe for her too, that the change might reinvigorate her. Through mutual friends, I followed her progress. Half a year later, I hired her back, and she was once again a joy to me and the company.

Max responded by saying that gifted bosses confirm what I learned from that experience: "The expression 'I had to fire her' is the right one. When there is *no other option*, and everybody knows it—boss, employee and coworkers—that's the right time. And when it's that time, the gifted boss–great employee alliances need not be ended, just suspended, a kind of workplace 'rain delay.' As we shall see in a minute, boss-employee alliances have a way of realigning, often lasting a lifetime."

Interconnected Careers

★ ★ ★ ★ ★

Now, as you may recall," Max said gently, "I'm not a fan of lifetime employment, or the old corporate pyramid. Still, it saddens me to see the decline of the old corporate loyalty, mostly because of what came next. What replaced it?"

It took me a minute to realize he was waiting for an answer. "Greed, self-interest, politics."

"Yes, instead of replacing lifetime employment with the joy of discovery, we got instead the fear of obsolescence. That's why alliances can be so soul satisfying. You make a permanent connection. Companies may come and go, but alliances endure." And he handed me the next principle.

> 6. An alliance between a gifted boss and a great employee is a kinship of talent, often creating a bond that can last a lifetime.

"A computer engineer named Dick Ruth," Max began, "who worked on a series of groundbreaking technical projects, like the Atlas missile guidance system and the Honeywell

6000, reflected back on his long career and how he kept intersecting the same individuals and said, 'There's a national—no, international—brotherhood of mavericks, and they find and refind each other.' Those are his words—the 'brotherhood of mavericks.' Sounds like a union for nonjoiners. And it will also sound familiar to gifted bosses and great employees, who without ever signing up, have become part of a talent union."

Max leaned in, gathering his intensity. "A computer systems engineer, Arno Rite, gave me an example of interconnected careers that I have in my memory. . . . Did I tell you that I have a photographic memory?"

"No more same-day service," I said, chuckling. "Yes."

He winked at me. There aren't too many people who can wink and make it seem natural, but Max was one. "Anyway, it went something like this." He took out a piece of paper and wrote the process. I've added some notes to replace his running commentary. It isn't important to follow the convolutions, just to accept the fact that such convolutions exist.

STEP ONE

- Rite takes a job at AMERCO (parent company for U-Haul and some smaller companies). New to management, he starts to build a department.

- He inherits Employee A.

- Then he hires Employee B (at urging of Employee A).

- Then he hires Employee C (via internal hire).

STEP TWO

- Employee B gets a new job at MicroAge (a Fortune 500 computer sales company), a promotion to department head.

- Soon after starting, Employee B convinces MicroAge to bring in Rite as head of a different department.

- Rite joins the company, and soon after, he brings over Employee C.

STEP THREE

- Employee C leaves to work for a MicroAge client.

STEP FOUR

- Rite and Employee C both leave their jobs in order to join together and create a new start-up, Dolphin Systems.

After finishing, Max said, "Let me pause to give you a substory that is very relevant to your situation. Rite should never have hired the person I've been calling 'Employee C.' Rite had a job opening at AMERCO and had several internal candidates who wanted to fill it. One of these was the obvious choice— highly qualified, technically superior to the others, and due for a promotion. Internal politics left no other option. But Rite had spotted a great employee, another internal candidate, one with far less technical knowledge and less tenure, but who had more personality, creativity and zest."

Max held up both index fingers, saying, "Corporate politics demanded the first candidate; Rite wanted the second one. So Rite decided that if he didn't like the results of the hiring process, he should change the process. He added a new step and had the two 'finalists' come back to take a 'what if?' test of various difficulties that could be encountered on the job. Selecting the scenarios carefully, he was able to weight them to the talents of the great employee, rather than to the skills of the more experienced candidate. And so he gathered 'proof' that the great employee was also the better candidate."

Max then explained that many of the most thoroughly intertwined careers were in technical fields, where the available pool of employees is limited. But alliances exist in every field and often result in careers that reunite. He told me of the career of a lawyer we've discussed earlier, Nancy Loftin. When she was working for the Securities Division of the Arizona Corporation Commission she hired a new staff member right out of law school. Her instincts were correct about him, and when she resigned to spend time with her new baby, he was promoted to her old job.

Later, when she was ready to restart her career, he hired her to work for him.

Both eventually left the Corporation Commission: he to join a large law firm in San Francisco; she to become the chief legal counsel for a large utility company, APS. When he later visited her, he admitted that the law firm life was a disappointment. As soon as she had an opening, she offered him a job, and he accepted.

Max gave me other examples, most so Byzantine that I won't attempt to recreate them here. Listening to him, I realized that I had encountered such alliances in my own work, I'd just never stopped to analyze them. For instance, I'd met an ad agency creative director named Richard Calvelli (whose credits include "I love what you do for me...Toyota" and "How do you spell relief?"). He spoke to me of working with a mutual friend, Steve Patchen. On three occasions Calvelli got a new job and each time started a campaign for the new company to hire Steve, not only to have a pal around but also because he knew he could count on his old friend to create the environment for truly creative advertising to take place.

Max summed up the examples by saying, "What these stories of interlocking careers make clear is that the selection of a boss is significant, often more significant than the choice of an employer company, perhaps more important than the choice of a career.

"I've been working for over fifty years, and one thing hasn't changed: the way most employees think about 'opportunities.' They tend to think almost exclusively of the job—and they evaluate that job mostly on the salary, maybe the title, maybe the benefits. Occasionally an employee will move up a level and consider the company or industry. Even so, this tends to be a surface analysis, thoughts such as 'It's working for a Fortune 500 company' or 'It's a chance to get out of banking.' Rarely is the boss a factor in the job decision, unless the person has experienced a great one. That made sense in the postwar hierarchical corporation, in which an employee would move within the organization and have many bosses, often more than one in a year. But it no longer makes sense, especially for talented employees. By choosing a gifted boss, they assure that their talents will be developed, and they gain an ally who may figure in their careers for a lifetime."

And then Max made some comments that struck me as particularly helpful. He said, "When employees hear about the latest panacea—networking, networking, networking—they naturally tend to think of the dreary business card exchanges at professional organizations and service clubs. But if the same amount of energy were devoted to maintaining relationships with former employers and coworkers, it would yield far more opportunities. There is a tendency for everyone at companies to forget those who leave. The departed person first gets blamed, and then gets forgotten. And someone who leaves a company will rarely see those left behind. But the gifted boss never forgets a great employee and maintains contact."

I thought of Max's earlier example, Dave Ridley, the VP of marketing for Southwest Airlines who hired a young intern two years after the internship ended.

"This also suggests," Max said, "that the wise employee will take every opportunity to display his or her talents within the company and the industry, especially where gifted bosses might see them. The alliances often start long before the actual boss-employee relationship. And, as we have seen, often continue after it. They exist on a separate plane, a kind of family—connected not by blood but talent."

And Max concluded with a quote from Dan Schweiker, the CEO of China Mist Tea. Commenting on the "family" relationship with his employees, he offered a different metaphor: "With the disintegration of families, people join companies like ours for the same reason that inner-city kids join gangs. They want to belong. It's that same feeling here, but you live longer. We have retirement benefits."

Conclusions

✮ ✮ ✮ ✮ ✮

Max rummaged around in his leather portfolio and handed me a sheet of paper. It was the "Six Realities of Gifted Bosses and Great Employees." And he handed me a couple of other pages, saying as he did, "These 'realities' suggest new leadership methods as well as new career strategies. So I couldn't resist writing up a few suggestions on applying those principles."

Here's what those pages contained:

- The hiring process is not passive—the employer isn't engaged in "sorting" but "spotting." Then, once spotted, the talented employee must be courted. (After all, these are *great* employees—they are likely to be treated well and paid well.) The gifted boss creates an exceptional environment and uses it to romance the great employee.

- Hiring is rarely based on just a job interview or referral—both sides understand that these are artificial. They want to see the other person's work, and the person at work, to see if they are talent "kin."

- Given the benefits of the alliance, having the right boss may be more important than the right company or even the right job.

- Given the importance of a gifted boss/great employee alliance, and the fact that such alliances begin outside the job market, new methods are demanded of individuals who want to emulate the success of talented individuals.
    - For bosses, the findings suggest that they deemphasize the traditional job market and instead increase opportunities to see talent in action.
    - Once talent is identified, great bosses learn the skills of bringing it inside—sometimes taking years, sometimes involving the creation of special projects, occasionally requiring "warehousing," "moles" or other unusual tactics.
    - As for employees, the talent-mating approach would suggest that they seek to broaden the number of people with whom they work, inside and outside the company, putting their talents on display in personal "product demonstrations." And whereas managers have traditionally done "empire building," the employee undertakes a similar strategy of "audience building."

I looked up from reading his summaries. "And with that," Max said, slumping back in his chair, feigning exhaustion, "you have sucked my brain dry. I don't have another thought left. Do not ask me any more questions."

I grinned and asked a question: "What should I do first?"

He flopped around, trying to reslump. "More, more, more. That's all I hear from you."

"I guess I'll just have to go back and fire the entire staff and start over," I said to tweak him.

But he was already working his way up, drawn irresistibly to my question.

"Okay, okay. Here's what I'd do. I would *not* start firing people, at least not yet. You haven't worked at being a gifted boss, so don't expect to have employees suited to a gifted boss. But I'd say you ought to let them know they are about to experience a dramatic break from the past."

"A set of experiments," I added, knowing that concept was important to Max.

"Yes, you might pick a dozen things that will make your division exceptional, make it magnetic. I don't know your kind of work well enough to tell you just what to do, but the list would surely include these:

- "You'd start by replacing rules with standards. For your department, you'd have to figure out what makes a great report or a great presentation—quality, creativity, speed, whatever. Your best becomes your norm. If you had a list of the five traits of a great presentation, and scored each one, that alone would change the way everyone works.

- "You insist that your employees stop coming to you for solutions, but that they become experts on options. I'd make a motto out of 'Show me the possibilities.'

- "You might also work with each employee to develop a personal 'brand.' Insist that each one have a specialty.

The typical performance review dwells on weaknesses, and the result is that everyone moves toward average on all traits. But a performer becomes great by having a great strength. Dwell on those.

- "And, most important, 'give 'em something to talk about.' You need a departmental strength to dwell on. Remember the poetry readings. You need to find your poetry. Maybe you collect reports from outside your industry and analyze them together. Or maybe you take the department on field trips to other corporations to learn what they do, and you adapt the best ideas. Maybe you bring in an acting coach to work with your employees on presentation skills. I'm not sure what it is for you, but find your poetry.

- "And through all these experiments, remember the goal is to make your group into **The Best Place for the Best People to Work.**"

There was a long silence as Max waited for me and my note taking to catch up. As I wrote out those suggestions, I realized that I could implement them and some other experiments within a week or two. And I could predict which of the employees would embrace these experiments and which would be heel draggers. In fact, I was already looking forward to scaring off a couple of the slackers. I said to Max, "By the time I get off the plane this evening, I'll have the list ready. And I know who I'll need to get rid of too."

"Don't be too sure," Max warned. "Some will surprise you. And I hope you'll have learned something about 'outplacement,' about graceful departures."

"Absolutely. Our corporation has good internal job movement. And thinking of myself as an 'outplacer' will remove some of my guilt feeling and make it easier to raise my standards and not keep putting off the need to get rid of the lackluster employees."

"Good. And then there's the hiring."

"I am now a talent scout. I am going to track every great employee in my field and even some outside it. I'm not going to wait for employees to hunt for a job with me, I'm going to get out and hunt them."

"Perfect. And I'd like to see you start to pay attention to new role models—agents, football coaches, heads of sales operations. For example, last time I visited my stockbroker I stopped to meet the man who heads the office, and I asked how he hires the top-producing brokers, something for which he is famous. He said this: 'I make it my business to know every top broker in town.' And then he said, 'The best ones, the ones I'd like to hire, I "drip on."' He explained what he meant by saying that he calls them once every month or two, or sends them an article. He said, 'I don't talk them into moving to my office, but I want *them* to talk to *me* if they start to think about moving.'"

Max added, "At first I disliked that notion of 'dripping,' but it's stuck with me. Here's the lesson: It's not enough to know who they are, but they have to know who you are. You might occasionally invite them to one of the events you put on, whatever your version of the poetry reading ends up being."

I was still writing furiously. Max laughed, and said, "Look at how serious we've gotten. Speaking of role models, take the coach of the University of Colorado football team, Rick Neuheisel, who is creating a self-perpetuating flow of recruits. Neuheisel was criticized for taking his team on ski trips, and thus risking injuries. His response was, 'My fear isn't that players get hurt. My fear is that players don't have fun, don't have a great time here. I want everyone who plays for me to want his son to play for me.'" Max grabbed my knee, and I realized it was still sore from yesterday.

"I don't know about your employee's offspring working for you," Max said, "but it's got to be fun. If you don't walk through your department and hear laughter, then you're not doing it right. When people are doing what they do best, they feel a special energy that comes close to giddiness. That could be one standard you put on yourself—you walk the halls and count how many laughs you hear."

I wasn't sure if Max was kidding or not, but I wrote it down, thinking that maybe I'd get a collection of quote books and joke books for the department and start making humor a part of our presentations. And I wondered aloud if I'd have the guts to create a standard for laughs-per-hour for presentations.

He beamed at me and said, "The hardest part is over. You've broken that glass rut. Instead of thinking about what you have to do, you're thinking about all you could do."

"One thing more," I said. "What about finding a gifted boss?"

"Ah, yes. We mustn't overlook the other side of our coin. All that you're doing here is going to make you visible. Remember: The gifted bosses are hunters. You're going to be a much bigger target after today."

"I understand," I replied, "but shouldn't I do more than wait?"

"Well, you're hardly waiting. We just talked about how you can help your current employees be great, and you need to do the same for yourself—you'll be working on your strength, finding your poetry, and you'll be known for your creative options. But you'll also be searching the company, the city, the country, maybe the world, for ideas on how to improve your work. And that means you'll meet some gifted bosses. And then you can make yourself available."

"Available?"

"Don't be coy. In fact, I bet there's a gifted boss somewhere in your corporation that you know."

"There is one man I'd love to work for."

"And I imagine that everyone in the company says dreamily, 'I'd love to work for him.' And maybe one in a hundred will actually make it happen."

He could see the puzzled look I had on my face.

"See what I've done," Max moaned. "I've done just what I've told you not to do in your department. I'm handing you answers instead of forcing you to create options. So you tell me: How could you get him to hire you?"

"First, I suppose I would need to get to know him. But, no, not just *know* him. I would need for him to see my work. And so I could find what companywide projects he's working on and try to represent our division."

"And?"

"I could ask him to speak to our group. I know he does 'brown bag lunches' for his employees and has speakers, maybe he'd come visit us. And he could learn about all our experiments."

"You've got it. Once you start to look, the ways present themselves. And then, when you develop some sort of ongoing relationship, you 'drip' on him. And eventually you get invited in. I met a man who wanted to work for a boss he admired. They had both worked in the same corporation, but she had moved on and eventually got to be the president. He had kept in touch, and so it was perfectly natural that he called to congratulate her on the new job. She says, 'I wish you were going to be there.' And he says, 'Maybe we could make that happen.' And two weeks later, he's the vice president."

★ ★ ★ ★ ★

"That's all. I'm finished. You're on your own."

Max fell back in his seat, a kid in an aging body, fizzing with the wisdom of nearly eight decades of curiosity. I thought of where we had begun this conversation, how heavy my heart had been, wondering if I could find meaning in my work, and if I couldn't, how could I find meaning in my life? And here I sat, knowing that I was no longer working for my salary but working on finding my poetry. I was no longer just shoring up my little weaknesses, I was evolving my strengths. And I no longer felt lonely in the postloyalty world, because I knew that I was going to develop alliances. I already had a great employee and gifted boss—Wild Brains—waiting to be courted.

I sat staring off up toward the tall cactuses, thinking these thoughts. When I glanced over at Max, I saw him staring at me paternally, and then a suspicion came over me: He was a gifted boss who was bringing me along, who was turning me into a great employee, worthy of his company.

I smiled, and he did a couple of Groucho eyebrow raises and said, "I'll get the car. There's one last stop before we're done."

The chairs were deep and angled back, so Max reached out a hand, saying, "Help me up." I took his hand with both of mine, and then he added his other hand around mine. After he rose, I held on for a moment in this four-hand shake, and he winked his wink and he laughed that laugh and we stood a minute, only connecting.

Epilogue

★ ★ ★ ★ ★

My return flight was scheduled for midday, twenty-four hours after I'd landed, just as Max had suggested. As we drove, I realized I was eager to return to the office. It had been a while since I'd had that feeling.

But Max had one last surprise for me, one last lesson about what I might strive to create in a workplace.

We drove to a newly built industrial area not far from the airport. Max was in Phoenix on business for one of the companies he owned, but he had promised some friends at a company called Insight that he would come by. When he picked Phoenix as the spot for our rendezvous, this was the event that he had wanted me to see.

We started with a tour of the building, the one Max had described for me the day before that is shaped like a giant X, which forces employees to converge in a pedestrian roundabout in the middle. But there were few employees converging, not that morning. We went back to the entrance we'd come through half an hour earlier. Before it had been mostly empty, but now we joined a crowd of hundreds of employees. And there we found two barbers, shaving heads.

It turns out that one of the key employees, Jon Moss, had battled Hodgkin's disease and won, and was ready to get back to work. When his return had been scheduled a couple of weeks back, one of Moss's coworkers went to the company's young CEO, Eric Crown, and explained that his department wanted to do something special for the return. And since Moss had lost his hair, thanks to the chemotherapy, some of them were planning to shave their heads, assuming Eric didn't mind. Not only didn't he mind, he suggested that the company donate a hundred dollars to the American Cancer Society for each shaved head. And Eric said that he would join in, on the condition that his would be the hundredth head shaved.

I chatted with one young man who was putting his name on a list for the barbers, and he commented, "I'm signing away my hair . . . and my social life." Nearby, a thoughtful soul was handing out packets of sunblock, to prevent those pale scalps from getting sunburned after work.

It took a while, but when the head count reached one hundred, a chant went up for the CEO's head: "ER-IC, ER-IC, ER-IC." And when he took his turn, the crowd, turning giddy by then, hooted and cheered for him at a startling volume. And even after his head was glistening, still the line continued. The final count was 192, including four women.

Then the word came that Moss was going to address us. I imagined how strange this would be for him, to return to work after many weeks, and to come into this room and see the banners and all those shaved heads.

He went to the front, a slender man of perhaps thirty years, with dark eyes, wearing an Insight shirt and a shy grin, and as he reached the front, a great cheer rose up from the crowd. He was stunned and moved—you could see the emotions pass over him—knocked back and pulled forward.

He eventually said a few words of thanks, all but speechless, and then he passed among them, feeling their bald heads, and they feeling his, every eye wet.

Max and I stood to the side, silent. Then he put his arm around my shoulder and whispered, "Oh, my... This is... No Ordinary Workplace."

We were quiet on the way back to the airport, minds and hearts full. When he dropped me off, his rental car idling at the departures ramp, Max got out to give me one last hug and a final shoulder squeeze. Just before he turned to go, he promised to come visit later in the year. Then, as he ducked inside the car he called back to me, "I'll know where to find you—out where the Wild Brains roam." And he laughed his barking laugh. I watched him pull away, vowing to myself to make it true.

Acknowledgments and Sources

★ ★ ★ ★ ★

This book is a collection of the wisdom of gifted bosses, and I thank them for their generosity, their kindnesses and ready laughter. Never has my research been such a joy.

As I sat down to write a bibliography, I realized that I didn't need one—with the exception of a few short quotations, all of the stories and examples were told to me by gifted bosses, either specifically for this book or during interviews for one of my newspaper columns. Instead, what is called for is an explanation. My task was to organize gifted boss stories, striving to create a book worthy of their wisdom. The best way to do so, I decided (thanks to the tough-love counsel of Kim Sauer of the Margret McBride Literary Agency), was to put them in the form of a conversation. If I wrote it well, perhaps you will be a bit disappointed to learn that it did not happen in just one day. Yes, there is a Max—his personality is that of my friend Roger Axford, a retired college professor and full-time eccentric. I used Roger's personality as a conduit to express what I'd learned. The book's other character is me, and also (I hope) you—Everymanager. All the stories within the story are true and merely rearranged to fit into a conversation.

In addition to all the gifted bosses who appear in this book, my thanks to Norm Stoehr, Steve Brown, Bob Nelson, Steve Patchen, Jim Fickess, Richard Gooding, Roger Axford and many Dautens: Jeri, Sandy, Hilary, Trevor and both Joels. Also, I am grateful to my agent, Margret McBride, and her team; and to my editor, Henry Ferris, and the folks at William Morrow.

A Note to the Reader

★ ★ ★ ★ ★

If you would like more of Max, you can find him in my previous book, *The Max Strategy*, also published by William Morrow. I wrote it for those who have grown bored or frustrated in their careers and who find themselves saying, "I don't know what I want to do when I grow up." If that's you, Max is ready to talk.

The next time you're on the Internet, stop by and visit at www.dauten.com. If you have questions, comments or stories, please write me at dale@dauten.com.